100 INCREDIBLE FACTS ABOUT HORSES

By Marc Dresgui
Illustrations by Laure Petit

Index

*"Being happy on horseback is
being between heaven and earth,
at a height that doesn't exist"*

— Jérôme Garcin

Introduction

Horses have been with humans for a very long time, but they still hold a great deal of mystery. Behind their strength, speed, and beautiful mane lie amazing talents that aren't always obvious at first glance. As you open this book, you'll discover a sensitive, intelligent animal full of surprises—quite different from the image we sometimes imagine.

You'll learn how its ears move almost like antennae, why its hooves are so ingenious, how its body adapts to cold, heat, or difficult terrain, and how it understands the world around it. Each fact has been chosen to show you that the horse isn't just elegant. It's also remarkably well-built.

As you turn the pages, you'll also see that horses live in groups, learn through trust, and recognize sounds, places, and even certain expressions. You'll meet sturdy ponies, endurance champions, clumsy yet courageous foals, and horses with unique personalities. Each has its own way of moving, observing, communicating, and growing.

I hope this book inspires you to look at horses with even more curiosity. Whether you already know a little about them or are just discovering them, you'll find something to marvel at in every chapter. So get ready to gallop off into a fascinating world, where every detail tells a true and surprising story.

Chapter 1 : Anatomy and Physical Characteristics

Fact 1 - Horses can move their ears

In horses, ears aren't just for hearing. They also move in almost every direction, much like little living antennas. Thanks to highly precise muscles, each ear can pivot to pick up a different sound. This is very useful in the wild, since horses often need to quickly detect what's happening around them.

A horse can turn its ears forward, to the sides, or backward without needing to move its entire head. This allows it to listen in multiple directions almost simultaneously. When a bird flies off behind it or another horse moves in the distance, its ears sometimes react even before its eyes look in that direction.

These movements also serve to show how the horse is feeling. Ears pointed forward often indicate that the horse is alert or curious. If they turn gently to the side, the horse may be relaxed. When laid back, they often signal irritation or anxiety. Riders therefore learn to observe the ears to better understand their horse.

Each ear has many muscles, giving the horse great precision. In humans, ears move very little, but for horses, they are almost part of their body language. This is a tremendous advantage for an animal that often lives in groups, in wide-open spaces, where hearing quickly can help keep them safe.

The next time you see a horse, take a good look at its ears before you even look at its hooves. You might notice that they turn, stop, and then move in another direction, as if searching for invisible messages. This small detail reveals a lot and shows just how sensitive, alert, and surprisingly expressive horses are.

Fact 2 - A horse's hoof acts as a natural shock absorber

When a horse gallops, its entire body moves forward with force, but it's not just its legs that absorb the impact. At the end of each l , the hoof plays an amazing role. It protects the foot, of course, but it also acts as a natural shock absorber. With every step, it helps the horse distribute its weight gently.

The hoof is not just a hard block, like a wooden shoe. It consists of a solid wall, but also of more flexible parts that work together. When the foot touches the ground, the hoof deforms slightly. This tiny movement helps distribute pressure and limit the jolts that travel up the leg.

Inside, everything is designed to help the horse move. In particular, there is a flexible structure called the foot pad, which helps absorb impacts. Thanks to this ingenious system, the foot does more than just support the body. It also helps protect the bones, joints, and tendons when the horse walks, trots, or runs.

This system is very useful, as a horse can weigh several hundred pounds. Without a foot capable of cushioning impacts, every stride would be much more tiring. This is also why the condition of the hooves is so important. A well-maintained hoof allows the horse to move more comfortably and maintain good balance on various terrains.

When watching a horse run, we often think of its speed or power. Yet part of the secret lies right at the bottom, in its hooves. These amazing feet work nonstop to protect its body with every movement. Beneath their simple appearance, they reveal a very clever natural mechanism, almost like a living cushion under each leg.

Fact 3 - A horse's legs are built to run long distances

When you watch a horse gallop, you mainly notice its speed. Yet its legs aren't just designed for speed. They also help it cover long distances without tiring too quickly. Over thousands of years, the horse's body has adapted to running, with long, strong, and lightweight limbs that are highly efficient over long distances.

A horse's legs are remarkable because their lower sections contain very few large muscles. Instead, they consist mainly of tendons and ligaments, much like powerful, flexible ropes. This structure makes the limbs lighter and requires less energy to move them. As a result, the horse can take thousands of strides with great efficiency.

Its long bones act like large levers. With each stride, they allow the horse to cover a lot of ground without wasting energy. The horse also places its feet in a very coordinated manner, which makes its gait more even. Its entire body participates in this movement, but the legs play the leading role, like four springs capable of propelling the animal far ahead.

This ability was of great help to humans in the past. Riders, messengers, and travelers relied on horses capable of enduring long journeys on roads, plains, or steppes. Some breeds are even famous for their remarkable endurance. The Arabian horse, for example, is known for covering very long distances, even under difficult conditions and on demanding terrain.

The horse's true prowess, therefore, lies not only in a quick start or a spectacular gallop. It also lies in its ability to endure. Its legs are built to keep moving forward, with power, flexibility, and consistency. Behind every stride lies a marvel of living mechanics, fine-tuned by nature to go ever further.

Fact 4 - The neck helps the horse maintain its balance

The horse's neck is the large, muscular section connecting its head to its body. It serves not only to support the head or graze on grass. It plays a very important role in balance. When the horse walks, trots, or gallops, its neck moves constantly to help it distribute the weight of its entire body more effectively.

As the horse moves forward, its body must remain stable despite changes in speed, turns, and uneven ground. Its neck then acts somewhat like a tightrope. By moving forward, rising, or leaning slightly, it helps the horse adjust its position. This movement seems simple, but it requires very precise coordination between muscles, bones, and joints.

This role becomes even more apparent when the horse turns, jumps, or descends a slope. In these moments, it must precisely coordinate its entire body to maintain stability. The neck supports this effort by shifting some of the weight forward or backward. It also helps the horse maintain a supple posture, making its movements more harmonious.

The head and neck work together like a natural pendulum. In such a large animal, this system is very useful. It allows for better control of the body's direction and adapts the posture to each situation. This is also why a horse needs freedom in its neck. A stiff neck hinders its movements and can make it harder to maintain balance.

The next time you see a horse moving, take a close look at its neck rather than just its legs. You'll see that it moves in perfect sync with each stride, almost as if it were dancing. This large, living pendulum helps the horse stay stable, supple, and elegant. Behind its beautiful silhouette lies a clever secret, essential to every one of its movements.

Fact 5 - A horse's teeth often reveal its age

In horses, teeth are a bit like a hidden calendar in the mouth. They change over the years, and experts can use them to estimate the animal's age. It's not secret magic, but careful observation. By looking at which teeth are present, worn down, or missing, we can already uncover valuable clues.

A young horse doesn't immediately have the same set of teeth as an adult. Just like with children, it starts with baby teeth, and then permanent teeth gradually appear. This replacement follows a fairly regular pattern. That's why the age of a foal or a young horse can often be estimated with fairly good accuracy.

In adults, observation becomes more challenging, but it remains useful. Teeth wear down from cutting grass and chewing hay. Their shape changes slowly, their surface alters, and certain small landmarks appear or fade over time. Experts therefore examine wear, inclination, and overall shape to form an opinion.

However, we must remain cautious. Teeth do not always reveal an exact age, like a date written on an ID card. Diet, soil type, or the care a horse receives can influence how much its teeth wear down. A horse that eats under specific conditions may have teeth that are more or less worn than those of another horse of the same age.

Looking at a horse's teeth is therefore a bit like reading the story of its growth. We see its transition from foal to adult, then the traces of time passing. This subtle detail reminds us of a fascinating fact: the body often retains the memory of the years. In horses, this memory lies hidden behind the lips, quietly stored away.

Fact 6 - A horse's eyes give it a very wide field of vision

A horse's eyes are positioned on the sides of its head, and this detail makes all the difference. Thanks to this position, it can see almost everything around it without turning its head. This is very useful for an animal that needs to quickly spot movement. In the wild, being able to see better around you can help you stay calm and safe.

This very wide view is called a wide field of vision. The horse can monitor what's happening in front, to the sides, and even partially behind it. However, there are also small areas it sees less clearly, right in front of its nose and just behind its hindquarters. It must then move its head slightly to better understand what's happening.

Horses don't see the world exactly the way we do. Because their eyes are set far apart, they often see a different image with each eye. In the area directly in front of them, the two images converge more, which helps them judge certain distances better. This becomes invaluable when they need to move forward with precision or clear an obstacle.

Its large eyes also pick up on movement very well. A slight movement in the grass or a figure passing in the distance can catch its attention very quickly. That's why a horse often notices details that humans miss. This visual sensitivity is part of its incredible alertness and also explains why certain sudden changes can startle it.

When you look at a horse, you first notice its size, its mane, or its strength. Yet its eyes already tell a large part of its story. They offer it a vast view of the world, almost like two open windows on either side of its head. With them, the horse doesn't just look far away; it watches over the space like a true sentinel.

Fact 7 - A horse's skin is sensitive to the slightest touch

A horse's skin is not just a simple covering. It is a highly sensitive organ, capable of detecting the slightest touch—a fly landing or a hand gently gliding over its neck. This sensitivity helps the horse better understand its surroundings. Even a slight shiver or a tiny vibration can immediately catch its attention.

You may have seen a horse quiver its skin without moving the rest of its body. This quick movement often allows it to shoo away an insect resting on its flank or shoulder. This is very practical, as flies and horseflies can be bothersome. Its skin thus functions somewhat like a living alarm, always ready to react.

This high sensitivity also plays a role in their interactions with other horses. In a herd, they sometimes touch each other with their noses, shoulders, or lips. These contacts convey calm, reassuring, or sometimes firmer messages. With humans as well, horses are highly sensitive to caresses, pressure, and gentle gestures, which requires a great deal of gentleness.

Certain areas are even more sensitive than others, such as the flanks, lips, or the inner thighs. This is why a rider can guide a horse with small, very subtle cues. A light pressure from the leg or hand may be enough. The horse responds not only to force, but above all to precision.

Beneath its powerful appearance, the horse thus hides incredible finesse. Its skin allows it to sense the world with astonishing precision, almost as if its entire body were listening to its surroundings. This detail reminds us of something important: a large animal can be very delicate. In the horse, strength and sensitivity go hand in hand in beautiful harmony.

Fact 8 - The mane also protects the neck from insects

A horse's mane often catches the eye, as it gives its silhouette a noble and elegant air. Yet it is not there solely for beauty. These long hairs growing along the neck can also serve a practical purpose. They form a sort of natural curtain that helps keep insects away from the neck.

On sunny days, flies, horseflies, and other small pests often swarm around horses. The neck is an exposed area, especially when the animal is grazing peacefully in a pasture. The mane can then limit their access to the skin somewhat. It doesn't replace the tail, of course, but it adds useful protection.

When the wind blows or the horse moves, the hairs of the mane quiver and shift constantly. This movement can disturb insects trying to land. It's a bit like a flexible, living barrier. Plus, the mane covers part of the skin, making it harder for insects to bite in the protected areas.

Nature often likes to combine several functions in a single feature. The mane helps protect, but it also contributes to each horse's appearance. Depending on the breed, it can be long, thick, wavy, or more subtle. On some horses, it falls to one side, while on others, it seems to almost dance around the neck.

The next time you see a mane flowing as a horse walks, think about all the things it does quietly. It's not just there to make the animal look majestic. It also helps with its day-to-day sur , keeping pesky little insects at bay. Here's yet another clever example of a detail that's both beautiful and useful.

Fact 9 - A horse's tail serves a purpose far beyond just looking pretty

A horse's tail is magnificent when it flows in the wind, but it's not just a pretty ornament. It serves several very useful purposes in daily life. The most obvious is warding off insects. With a single swift movement, a horse can shoo away flies resting on its flanks, legs, or hindquarters.

This large natural fly swatter works almost nonstop on hot days. When the insects become too numerous, the tail springs into action with precision. It sweeps through the air, sometimes touching the skin, then moves away immediately. This gesture seems simple, but it helps the horse stay much calmer. Without this valuable aid, certain hours in a pasture would be far more unpleasant.

The tail also serves to show emotions and convey messages. A relaxed horse lets it move calmly, while an annoyed horse may swish it more nervously. In a herd, these movements are part of body language. They complement the position of the ears, head, and the rest of the body to express the current mood.

It even plays a small role in balance and movement. When the horse turns quickly, accelerates, or changes direction, the tail sometimes accompanies its movement like a light pendulum. It does not support the body, of course, but it follows the action and contributes to the harmony of its silhouette. In foals, too, it accompanies joyful runs and play.

Observing a horse's tail, then, is to observe a very clever tool hidden beneath an elegant appearance. It protects, it signals, and it naturally accompanies the body's movements. This detail, which we sometimes notice last, nevertheless reveals a great deal. In horses, even what seems decorative often serves a real purpose—discreet yet remarkable.

Fact 10 - The horse's skeleton combines strength and speed

Beneath a horse's skin and muscles lies a remarkable framework. Its skeleton supports the entire body, protects certain organs, and enables movement. But it doesn't just keep the animal standing. It is also designed to help it run with power and speed. Every bone contributes to this incredible living machine built to move forward.

A horse's legs are long and sturdy, with bones arranged to lengthen its stride. Thanks to them, the horse can cover a lot of ground in just a few steps. This is a valuable advantage for an animal that, in the wild, needed to be able to quickly escape danger. Its bone structure therefore helps it go fast, but also far.

The back and shoulders also play an important role. They transmit the body's force forward and support the movements of the legs. The pelvis, at the rear, helps generate the momentum needed to accelerate. One can think of the skeleton as a series of well-placed levers, capable of transforming the energy of the muscles into efficient movement.

Horses also have a remarkable feature. Unlike humans, they do not have a collarbone. Their shoulders are connected to the rest of their body primarily by muscles and ligaments. This gives them greater flexibility of movement and helps absorb shock while running. This anatomical structure makes their gallop smoother, more powerful, and better suited to exertion.

When a horse gallops, we often admire its speed without thinking about what lies beneath its coat. Yet its skeleton works tirelessly with every stride. It supports, guides, and transmits force with impressive precision. It is not a simple framework, but a natural structure of great intelligence, designed for power, balance, and momentum.

Chapter 2 : Senses and Communication

Fact 11 - Horses Are Good at Reading Facial Expressions

A human face conveys a great deal, even without speaking. A smile, a narrowed gaze, or furrowed brows already offer clues. Horses seem highly skilled at noticing these signals. Research has shown that they distinguish between different human expressions and do not view them all in the same way.

When a horse sees an angry face, its reaction may change. In some experiments, it looked at that face more quickly with its left eye—an interesting detail for this animal—and its heart rate increased more significantly. This suggests that it perceives the emotions visible on a human face better than one might think.

This ability isn't just for observing in the moment. Other studies have shown that horses can also remember an expression they've seen on a person before. Later, when faced with that same person with a neutral expression, they may react differently depending on the emotion they had previously detected. It's an astonishing ability.

Scientists have also discovered that horses combine multiple cues to understand human emotion. They don't just look at the face. They can also link an expression with a voice to form a more complete picture of a person's state. This demonstrates a great subtlety in how they perceive humans.

That's why so many riders and handlers try to approach horses calmly and gently. These large animals don't just notice sudden movements. They also pick up on subtle details in facial expressions and body language. Behind their large, calm eyes lies remarkable attentiveness—almost as if they were silently deciphering our emotions.

Fact 12 - A horse shows its mood with its ears

For horses, ears aren't just for hearing the sounds of the world. They're also part of their language. By watching them closely, you can often tell if a horse is curious, calm, uncomfortable, or annoyed.

This is very useful, since horses communicate mainly through their bodies. Their ears are therefore a bit like little living signs.

When the ears point forward, the horse is often paying attention to something. It is listening, observing, and trying to understand what has caught its attention. If they move in several directions, it is monitoring multiple sounds at once. When they are held more loosely at the sides, this may indicate a moment of relaxation, rest, or quiet reflection.

On the other hand, ears laid back often signal that it's best to be cautious. The horse may be annoyed, anxious, or unhappy with what's happening around it. This sign should never be ignored. It doesn't mean the same thing in every situation, but it clearly indicates that a strong emotion is present.

Horses have been using this language among themselves for a very long time. In a herd, each horse observes the others to understand the mood of the moment. A simple ear position can signal unease, tension, or sudden interest. With humans, too, this detail matters a great deal. Caretakers and riders learn to read it to better respect the animal.

Observing a horse's ears is, therefore, a bit like silently reading its thoughts. They turn, prick up, relax, or lie flat, and each of these positions tells a story. This small detail shows just how expressive the horse is. Even without words, it knows how to convey a wealth of emotions to those who take the time to observe it closely.

Fact 13 - A horse's nostrils detect a thousand scents

A horse's nostrils are much more than just two openings for breathing. They are at the heart of a sense of smell that is very useful in its daily life. Thanks to them, the horse detects the scent of grass, a , water, another animal, or a familiar human. Its nose thus helps it explore the world almost like a detective.

When a horse approaches something unfamiliar, it often begins by sniffing it. It extends its nose, inhales deeply, and then sometimes raises its head slightly to better analyze the scent. This habit allows it to gather a wealth of information without making a sound. A simple scent can already tell it whether the object, place, or animal seems familiar.

Smell also plays an important role among horses. They often recognize each other by scent and use it to better understand who is near them. A mare can recognize her foal this way, and horses within the same group exchange many invisible messages. Their noses thus become a very discreet communication tool.

The nostrils are also very mobile. They can flare to let in more air, especially during exertion, but they also serve to better detect certain scents. When a horse sniffs intently, its nostrils are actively working. This small movement, which we barely notice, actually hides a precise, rapid, and very useful observation in the horse's life.

When looking at a horse, we often admire its mane, hooves, or speed. Yet its nose also deserves our attention. Thanks to its nostrils, it smells, recognizes, compares, and understands a multitude of things we don't even notice. Beneath their simple appearance, they offer the horse a true, discreet superpower—one that is invaluable at every moment of its day.

Fact 14 - Horses also communicate through their posture

Horses don't use words, yet they understand each other very well. Their entire bodies serve to send messages. The position of the head, the angle of the neck, the way they stand or shift their weight already convey a great deal. In a herd, this discreet communication allows them to live together quietly and with great efficiency.

A horse that raises its head and extends its neck often indicates that it is observing something closely. Another horse that maintains a relaxed body , a supple neck, and calm limbs conveys a sense of relaxation. Conversely, a tense posture, with tight muscles and a body poised to move, may signal anxiety or strong irritation.

The distance between horses is also part of their language. A horse may take a confident step forward to ask another to move aside, without touching it. The other horse then understands the message through posture, gaze, and overall movement. In many cases, this simple gesture is enough to prevent a more dramatic conflict.

Foals learn to read these signals very early on. By observing their mother and other horses, they gradually discover the group's rules. This ability to read body language is essential for knowing when to approach, when to wait, or when to move away. With humans, too, a horse quickly notices whether a posture is calm, abrupt, hesitant, or reassuring.

Watching a horse is therefore a bit like witnessing a silent conversation. Without words or cries, it can convey its mood, ask for space, or show its trust. Its posture becomes a true living language—precise and elegant. The more we learn to observe it, the more we discover that its body speaks almost as clearly as a voice.

Fact 15 - A whinny can have several meanings

The neigh is undoubtedly the horse's most well-known call. When we hear it, we immediately think of a horse. Yet this sound doesn't always mean the same thing. Depending on the situation, it can express a call, an emotion, or a reaction to what's happening around it. A single sound can therefore tell several different stories.

A horse may neigh to call out to a companion it can no longer see. In a pasture, at the stable, or in the distance along a path, this call helps them stay in touch. It serves much like a voice carried by the wind. If a horse is separated from a friend or its herd, its neighing may become louder and more insistent.

Sometimes, a whinny also shows excitement or impatience. A horse that recognizes a familiar person, is waiting for its meal, or spots other horses may let out a happier cry. At other times, the sound may convey anxiety or a need for a response. What matters, then, is not just the cry itself, but also the context.

Horses don't just use neighing to communicate, by the way. They snort, whinny, move their ears, change their posture, and use their whole bodies to make themselves understood. Neighing is part of this whole. It's a very useful auditory signal, especially when distance prevents them from seeing each other. It then complements the messages sent by their gestures.

When you hear a horse neigh, imagine that it might be trying to say much more than just hello. It's calling, searching, reacting, or sharing an emotion. Its cry isn't a random noise. It's a living message, carried by its voice, which shows once again just how expressive and fascinating horses are.

Fact 16 - Horses Hear Very Subtle Sounds

Horses have very keen hearing, capable of picking up sounds that many humans barely notice. The rustling of grass, a distant footstep, or the faint clinking of a gate can already catch their attention. This ability is invaluable for an animal that has long had to monitor its surroundings. Hearing something early often means understanding what's approaching more quickly.

Their large, movable ears play a key role in this ability. Each ear can pivot almost independently of the other to pick up a sound coming from a specific direction. It's a bit like the horse has two adjustable microphones on its head. Thanks to this system, it can listen in front, behind, or to the side without moving its entire body.

This sensitivity also allows them to react very quickly. Even before a human has realized a sound exists, the horse may already have raised its head, fixed its gaze in a direction, and turned its ears toward the sound source. This reflex isn't mere nervousness. It's an intelligent way to check whether the sound signals something important or not.

In a herd, this attentive hearing also helps them stay connected with the other horses. A distant whinny, a sudden movement, or even the faint sound of hooves provides useful information. So the horse doesn't just listen to protect itself. It also listens to understand the world around it, almost as if reading an invisible newspaper made of sounds.

The next time you see a horse standing still with its ears pricked, don't assume it's doing nothing. It may be listening to a world of sound that we barely perceive. Behind its apparent calm, its ears are working with precision. This is yet another remarkable talent of this animal, always attentive, elegant, and wonderfully well-equipped to observe its world.

Fact 17 - A horse's eyes quickly detect movement

A horse's eyes are highly effective at spotting movement. Positioned on the sides of its head, they give it a very wide view of the world. Thanks to this positioning, it quickly notices movement in the grass, an animal in the distance, or a silhouette shifting position. This is a very useful ability for staying alert to its surroundings.

In the wild, this ability helps the horse react quickly even before fully understanding what's happening. A simple rustle, a swaying branch, or a bird taking flight can catch its eye. Its eyes are therefore less suited for reading small details up close than for monitoring movements around it. It mainly observes what changes suddenly within its field of vision.

This quickness explains why some horses seem surprised by things that appear trivial to humans. A bag moving in the wind, a shadow gliding across the ground, or a fluttering jacket can be enough to capture their attention. The horse isn't trying to overreact. It simply responds with a visual system highly trained to notice unusual movements.

Their large eyes also work in conjunction with their ears and posture. When they detect movement, they often turn their ears in the same direction, raise their neck, and prepare to observe more closely. Their entire body then participates in this rapid assessment. It is not just a casual glance, but a thorough check to understand what is happening.

When you see a horse suddenly fix its gaze on a specific spot, it may have spotted a moving detail that you haven't even noticed. Its eyes are remarkable motion detectors, always ready to pick up on the slightest change. This discreet talent reminds us that a horse is never truly inattentive. Even when calm, it maintains a silent and impressive watchfulness around itself.

Fact 18 - Touch is vital for the mare and her foal

From the very first moments, touch plays an immense role between a mare and her foal. Barely born, the foal feels the contact of its mother's muzzle on its body. She gently nudges it, sniffs it, and brushes against it with care. These gestures help it discover the world and understand that it is not alone.

This contact serves not only to reassure. It also helps the mare and her foal recognize each other very quickly. By touching it, sniffing it, and staying close to it, the mother memorizes its scent, its presence, and its reactions. For its part, the foal learns to recognize its mother's warmth, gentleness, and security.

In the hours following birth, the foal must already accomplish great feats. It tries to stand up, balance on its long legs, and find its mother's milk. Touch helps it through each of these stages. The mare can encourage it with small, gentle touches, almost as if she were showing it the way.

Later, this language of touch continues. The foal often stays close to its mother, walks by her side, and seeks her touch in new situations. A light pressure, a brush, or simply moving closer can already convey a message. Among horses, many important things are communicated this way—silently, through the body and presence.

This tactile bond shows just how delicate and precious the relationship between a mare and her foal is. Even before the foal can see clearly or fully understand what is going on, it learns through its mother's touch. In this silent dialogue, every gesture counts. It is beautiful proof that, for horses, tenderness can also be a great life lesson.

Fact 19 - Horses recognize certain voices

Horses don't just listen to the sounds around them. They can also recognize human voices and remember them. Studies have shown that they distinguish between different people using auditory cues, such as voice pitch. This means that a horse does not perceive all human voices as identical.

This ability becomes even more interesting when the horse already knows the person. Research has shown that it can associate a voice with a specific human, as if linking what it hears to a face, a presence, and a way of behaving. Its brain thus constructs a sort of complete portrait, made up of sounds and memories.

A horse's vocal memory also appears to be linked to its past experiences. In one study, researchers observed that horses reacted differently depending on whether the voice they heard had been associated with a positive or less pleasant experience. In other words, they don't just hear a voice. They also remember, to some extent, what it represents to them.

Other research even suggests that horses can combine what they hear with what they see. They can link certain human voices to specific faces or categories of people. This keen observation shows that their relationship with humans is more nuanced than one might think at first glance.

When a horse seems to react to a person before even seeing them, it may have recognized their voice. This subtle detail reminds us that they observe humans with great attention. Behind their large, mobile ears lies an astonishing memory, capable of recording familiar sounds and linking them to memories. It is a beautiful testament to their sensitive intelligence.

Fact 20 - A horse can signal danger without making a sound

In a herd, horses don't always need to neigh to understand each other. Sometimes all it takes is a glance, a posture, or a very subtle movement to signal that caution is needed. A horse that notices something strange may raise its head, freeze its body, and prick up its ears. The others immediately notice this change and become more vigilant.

This silent language works very well because horses spend a lot of time watching their companions' reactions. If one of them suddenly tenses up, the others understand that something warrants closer attention. They haven't seen the danger themselves yet, but they can already sense the unease in the first horse's demeanor. It's a quick and effective way to share a warning.

The position of the neck, the orientation of the ears, and the direction of the gaze already provide valuable information. A horse may also come to a sudden stop, shift its weight, or turn slightly toward the suspicious spot. These signals are almost invisible to us, but within the herd, they are very clear. Each animal then becomes more alert, without any need for a cry.

This discreet communication is very useful in the wild. Making too much noise could draw more attention to the group. Thanks to their silent gestures, horses can therefore warn one another while remaining cautious. It's a bit like everyone is constantly reading each other's body language. Their safety often depends on this keen observation and their ability to react together.

When you see several horses raise their heads at the same time, you're often witnessing this type of silent message. No words, no cries, and yet all the information is being conveyed. This ability shows just how attentive horses are to one another. In their world, silence isn't emptiness. On the contrary, it can be filled with subtle and highly intelligent signals.

Chapter 3 : Behavior and Intelligence

Fact 21 - Horses learn through repetition and trust

A horse does not learn like a student sitting at a desk, but it remembers very well what it experiences often. When a gesture, a command, or an exercise is repeated several times in a calm setting, it gradually understands what is expected of it. Repetition helps it memorize, recognize situations, and respond with greater precision.

This repetition works even better when the horse feels safe. If it is afraid, feels rushed, or does not understand, it learns less effectively. On the other hand, with a patient person, clear gestures, and a calm atmosphere, it becomes more attentive. Trust then acts as a key that unlocks the door to learning.

Horses also closely observe the consequences of their actions. If a correct movement brings comfort, rest, or a soothing voice, they are more inclined to repeat it. This isn't magic, but a smart way of associating an action with a result. Little by little, the exercise becomes simpler, almost second nature to them.

This is why people who work with horses often repeat the same basics. Moving forward, stopping, turning, yielding to light pressure, or staying calm in a new situation takes time. The horse progresses better when the requests remain consistent. Changing things too much, being too abrupt, or overcomplicating matters risks confusing the horse and making it hesitant.

Learning with a horse, therefore, isn't just about repeating an exercise over and over. It's also about building a solid relationship, where the animal feels understood and respected. When repetition meets trust, progress becomes more beautiful and more lasting. Behind every success, there is often this quiet alliance between patience, memory, and a shared bond.

Fact 22 - A horse knows how to solve small problems

The horse is not just a fast and powerful animal. It also knows how to think through small everyday situations. Faced with an easy obstacle, an unusual barrier, or a new object, it can observe, try, hesitate, and then find a simple solution. Its intelligence is not like that of humans, but it certainly exists.

For example, a horse sometimes understands that it must go around a blocked passage rather than insist on going straight through. It can also learn to gently push a poorly closed door with its nose, or to shift its body in a different way to reach some hay. These aren't complex calculations, of course, but they are already very useful little acts of reasoning.

To succeed, the horse relies mainly on its experience, memory, and powers of observation. It notices what works and what doesn't. If a solution brings it comfort or helps it achieve its goal, it tends to remember it. Gradually, it becomes more adept at handling certain simple challenges.

Not all horses react exactly the same way. Some are more curious and quickly seek a solution, while others remain more cautious and take more time. Temperament therefore plays an important role. A calm, confident horse often thinks more clearly than a stressed horse, because it can observe without rushing.

This talent shows that the horse does not merely follow habits. It can also adapt, test, and understand small new situations. Behind its large, calm gaze lies an attentive mind that learns from the world around it. It is a discreet yet very real intelligence that makes this animal even more fascinating to observe.

Fact 23 - Horses have an excellent sense of place

A horse does not pass through a place as if it were to forget it immediately. It often remembers paths, obstacles, turns, and even certain details of the scenery. This spatial memory is very useful for moving with confidence. In the wild as well as in human- , knowing how to find a path or recognize a place can save time and avoid much hesitation.

When a horse takes the same route several times, it eventually records it with precision. It can remember a gate, a watering hole, a shelter, or a shady spot. Even after some time has passed, it sometimes recognizes the place from the very first steps. Its body then seems to relax, as if it were returning to a place already stored in its memory.

This ability stems in part from its need to observe its surroundings carefully. The horse notices the contours of the ground, the placement of trees, the shape of a path, or the layout of a yard. It also memorizes pleasant or uncomfortable places. A calm, familiar, and reassuring place leaves a different impression than a narrow or unexpected passage.

Humans often benefit from this quality without even realizing it. A horse that knows its stable, pasture, or usual route well moves through them with greater confidence. It knows where to turn, where to stop, and sometimes even where it's going before being explicitly told. This shows just how quietly its memory works.

Behind its large, attentive ears and curious eyes, the horse thus builds a true map of the world around it. It doesn't just retain memories of sounds or smells. It also remembers places, paths, and landmarks. This is a valuable talent, making it a cautious, observant explorer with a remarkably reliable memory.

Fact 24 - In a herd, each horse often has its own role

A herd of horses is a bit like a very well-organized team. They all live together, but they don't do exactly the same thing at the same time. Some are more vigilant, others calmer, and still others lead the group as it moves. Without a vocal leader, each horse gradually finds its place through experience and habit.

In many groups, certain horses quickly notice changes in their surroundings. They lift their heads, observe, and listen, and the other s take note of their reaction. Others know how to calm the atmosphere with their quiet demeanor. There are also more assertive horses, capable of pushing a neighbor aside or guiding a movement. These aren't official positions, but they are very useful roles.

Mares, foals, and other horses do not always act the same way depending on their age, temperament, and place in the group. A young horse plays a lot and learns the rules of living together. An experienced adult is better at knowing the appropriate distances to maintain, body signals, and the right ways to stay calm.

These roles aren't set in stone like on a chart. They can change over time, with the arrival of a new horse, or in a specific situation. An animal that's very confident in a familiar pasture may become more cautious in an unfamiliar place. The herd is constantly adapting, like a small, living society where everyone watches each other closely.

When we watch horses together, we often see much more than just a group grazing. We discover a subtle organization, made up of glances, distances, and complementary behaviors. Each horse contributes something to the herd's balance. This communal life offers a beautiful lesson from nature: moving forward together becomes easier when everyone finds their place.

Fact 25 - Horses enjoy living with other horses

Horses are not meant to live alone. For a very long time, they have been accustomed to living in groups, surrounded by other horses. This communal life helps them feel safer and more at ease. In a herd, each horse observes the others, shares the same space, and benefits from a reassuring presence throughout the day.

When several horses live together, they do more than just stand side by side. They follow one another, watch each other, sniff one another, and communicate with very subtle gestures. One may sound the alarm, another may remain calm, and the whole group reacts. This social life plays a major role in their daily lives and their well-being.

Horses also enjoy physical contact. They may stand close to one another, walk together, and sometimes gently scratch each other's necks or backs with their teeth. This behavior, known as mutual grooming, helps strengthen their bonds. It's not just practical; it's also a way to relax and show trust.

A horse isolated for too long may feel uncomfortable, get bored, or become more nervous. It is then missing an important part of its natural life. Even if it enjoys human company, this does not completely replace the company of another horse. Nothing quite compares to a companion that speaks the same body language.

When we see horses grazing together in a pasture, we are witnessing something very important to them. They aren't just sharing a piece of land. They share a group life, made up of signals, habits, and presence. This brings to mind a simple and beautiful idea: for the horse, friendship and companionship are part of happiness.

Fact 26 - A stressed horse quickly changes its behavior

Stress in a horse is often visible very quickly, even if no sound signals it. A calm animal may suddenly raise its head, stretch its neck, open its eyes wider, or shift its body nervously. These changes are important to observe, as they show that the horse has noticed something that worries, bothers, or overwhelms it.

Its ears will then move more rapidly, its nostrils may flare, and its muscles may become more tense. Some horses will paw the ground, others will speed up their movements, or stare intently in a specific direction. They may also become more hesitant. These are not mere whims. Their bodies are simply reacting to prepare for a situation they perceive as threatening.

Stress can stem from a sudden noise, an unfamiliar object, separation from other horses, or a new environment. Since horses are highly attuned to changes in their surroundings, they quickly notice unusual details. Their behavior then adapts immediately . They seek to understand, protect themselves, or regain a sense of security.

Not all horses show their stress in the same way. Some become very agitated, while others freeze and appear almost motionless. Temperament, age, and past experiences play a major role. A horse accustomed to a situation will sometimes remain calmer, while another, less confident, will react much more quickly.

Observing these signs allows you to better help the horse at the right moment. A reassuring environment, calm gestures, and a patient attitude can help it regain its balance. Behind this rapid change in behavior, there is therefore a clear message. The horse isn't trying to make things difficult. It's simply showing that it needs to understand and be reassured.

Fact 27 - Young horses play to learn and grow

For young horses, play is not just a way to pass the time. It is a real-life outdoor classroom. By running, leaping, and chasing each other, foals discover their bodies, test their legs, and improve their balance. Behind their joyful antics, they are already learning essential skills for the rest of their lives.

When two young horses play together, they gently nibble at each other, push one another, circle around each other, and sometimes break into a gallop all at once. These games help them better coordinate their movements. They also learn to control their strength and react quickly. Every race becomes a training session disguised as a fun, energetic moment.

Play also helps them understand the rules of group life. By observing others' reactions, the foal discovers what it can do and what is best avoided. It learns to maintain a distance, to yield its place, or to invite a companion. Little by little, these interactions shape its social behavior and how it lives with other horses.

These joyful moments also build confidence. A curious young horse dares to explore, test, and try again. By playing in a safe environment, it discovers new sensations without feeling threatened. This helps it become more skilled and self-assured. Growing up, then, is not just about gaining height, but also about gaining experience.

Watching a foal play is like seeing nature preparing a future adult horse. Every jump, every turn, and every sudden start teaches it something useful. Beneath its appearance as a little acrobat, it is already building its strength, its agility, and its relationships with others. Play then becomes much more than just fun; it becomes a wonderful life lesson.

Fact 28 - Horses observe a lot before acting

Horses don't always act immediately. Very often, they start by looking, listening, and sensing their surroundings before deciding what to do. An unfamiliar object, a strange noise, or a change in the landscape first catches their attention. They then take a few moments to assess the situation. This caution helps them avoid many surprises.

When something intrigues it, the horse often raises its head, stretches its neck, and turns its ears toward whatever has caught its interest. Its eyes scan for the slightest movement, while its nostrils sniff the air. Its entire body seems to be asking a silent question. Before moving forward or backward, it first gathers information like a true investigator.

This habit is very useful for an animal that must remain vigilant. Observing before acting allows it to distinguish a real danger from a simple, insignificant detail. A moving branch, a tarp in the wind, or an animal in the distance do not all provoke the same reaction. The horse therefore quickly analyzes what it perceives before choosing its response.

This behavior also explains why some horses seem to hesitate when faced with something new. They aren't trying to disobey. Above all, they're taking the time to understand. A confident, calm horse often observes better and eventually moves forward more serenely. Human patience can be a great help here, as it gives the horse time to examine what's worrying it.

Watching an attentive horse is like seeing a cautious mind deep in thought. Nothing seems spectacular, and yet it is already gathering clues with its eyes, ears, and nose. This discreet talent reminds us of something important: wisdom does not always mean acting quickly. In horses, it often begins with calm, precise, and remarkably intelligent observation.

Fact 29 - Some horses are curious, others cautious

Not all horses react the same way to something new. Faced with a strange object, one might approach almost immediately, while another prefers to stop, look for a long time, and wait. This difference stems partly from their temperament. Just as with humans, some are naturally more daring, while others prefer to first make sure everything seems safe.

A curious horse often moves forward with its nose, pricks up its ears toward the new object, and tries to smell or observe it more closely. It wants to understand what is in front of it. A cautious horse, on the other hand, keeps its distance at first. It is no less intelligent; it simply chooses a different way to explore the world.

Past experiences also play an important role. A horse that has often discovered new places in a calm setting may become more confident. Conversely, a horse that has been startled several times by unsettling situations is likely to remain more wary. Temperament matters greatly, but memory, habit, and the atmosphere around it also shape how it reacts.

In a herd, these differences can be useful. The curious horse sometimes dares to go first, while the more cautious one observes the reactions before following. Together, they offer the group several ways to face the unknown. Nature often favors this variety, as it allows the herd to adapt better to the situations they encounter.

When you watch a horse hesitate or approach with a determined stride, you catch a glimpse of a small part of its personality. It's not just a minor detail. It's a genuine way of being in the world. Whether curious or cautious, every horse has its own unique style, and that's also what makes these magnificent animals so fascinating to observe.

Fact 30 - A horse's trust is built slowly

A horse's trust isn't earned in an instant. It's built little by little through calm gestures, reassuring habits, and repeated moments free of fear. A horse observes a great deal before granting its trust. It watches the voice, the movements, and the overall demeanor. For a horse, feeling safe always comes before everything else.

When a person acts gently and consistently, the horse begins to understand that they pose neither a sudden surprise nor a threat. The horse then retains the pleasant experiences and relaxes more easily. This progress is often subtle. A calmer gaze, a more relaxed posture, or a more confident stride already indicate that a bond is beginning to form.

Conversely, trust can be hindered if the horse experiences confusing or unsettling moments. Abrupt movements, poorly explained requests, or a stressful environment complicate the relationship. The horse isn't trying to be difficult; it's simply protecting its equilibrium. To move forward with it, therefore, requires patience, clarity, and a great deal of consistency.

This trust also grows through small successes. Approaching calmly, accepting a stroke, following a simple request, or staying relaxed in a new place are real steps forward. The horse then learns that certain unfamiliar situations can go well. Little by little, its confidence grows. What it feared yesterday sometimes becomes much easier today.

Building a horse's trust is a bit like building a solid bridge. You don't add everything all at once, but stone by stone. This work takes time, yet it yields valuable results. When the bond becomes strong, the horse becomes more serene, more attentive, and more responsive. Its trust grows slowly, but once it exists, it is remarkable.

Chapter 4 : Gaits and Movements

Fact 31 - The horse's walk is a calm and sure gait

The walk is the horse's calmest and most natural gait. When moving in this way, its four legs move one after the other in a very regular sequence. This steady rhythm conveys a sense of security and smoothness. It is often the gait observed when a horse is strolling leisurely, exploring a path, or beginning its work.

At this gait, the horse's body moves with suppleness, without sudden jolts. Its back moves with the motion, its neck sways slightly, and each stride seems well-placed. For the rider, too, the walk is distinctive, as it conveys a continuous rocking motion. It almost feels like being rocked, as if on a large, slow, and tranquil wave.

The walk is reassuring because it allows the horse to take the time to observe its surroundings. It can look, listen, smell, and think without rushing. This gait is ideal for exploring a new place or navigating difficult terrain. On rocky ground, through a narrow passage, or on a slope, the walk helps the horse stay cautious.

It is also an important gait for learning. Many young horses start with the walk when they are introduced to new commands. It gives them time to understand, adjust their balance, and coordinate their movements. Even for an experienced horse, this gait remains valuable. It is used to warm up, recover after exertion, or return to a peaceful rhythm.

When you see a horse walking, don't assume it's just doing something simple. It displays a form of calm, steady, and highly controlled elegance. Behind this peaceful gait lies a beautiful, precise, and harmonious mechanics. The walk reminds us that a horse doesn't need to run to impress. Sometimes, tranquility alone reveals all its beauty.

Fact 32 - The trot makes the rider's entire body bounce

The trot is a very distinctive gait in horses. It is faster than the walk but less vigorous than the gallop. When the horse trots, its legs move forward in diagonal pairs, creating an energetic and regular motion. For the rider, this gait is immediately noticeable, as it causes a much more pronounced bounce throughout the body.

With each stride, the horse pushes off its limbs with energy, and its back transmits this upward movement. The rider then feels a sort of repeated little bounce. This is neither a fault nor a strange jolt. It is simply the natural way the trot works, with an impulse that travels up through the saddle to the rider's torso.

This is why learning to follow the trot takes a bit of practice. The rider must find the right rhythm with their hips, legs, and back to avoid being jostled. Often, they discover the raised trot, a technique that involves rising slightly every other beat. This method helps to accompany the movement with greater suppleness.

For the horse, too, the trot is a useful and interesting gait. It allows the horse to move forward with energy while maintaining good regularity. Over many distances, it is a practical gait for moving efficiently. It also demonstrates the coordination of the entire body, as the back, neck, and legs work together like the parts of a finely tuned machine.

When a rider discovers the trot, they quickly realize that riding a horse is not just about sitting. You have to listen to the movement, follow it, and almost dance with it. This characteristic bounce then becomes a shared language between human and animal. Beneath its apparent simplicity, the trot reveals all the horse's liveliness and momentum.

Fact 33 - The canter is a very spectacular gait

Among the horse's gaits, the canter is undoubtedly the most impressive to watch. It conveys a sense of speed, power, and freedom. When a horse canters, its body seems to leap forward with great energy. Yet this movement is not disorderly. It follows a precise rhythm, organized into several beats, like a kind of living music.

When galloping, the legs do not all touch the ground at the same time. They strike the ground in a specific order, creating a three-beat gait, followed by a very brief moment when no hoof touches the ground. During this split second, the horse seems almost to fly. It is this detail that makes the gallop so spectacular and so different from other gaits.

The horse's entire body participates in this astonishing mechanics. The limbs propel the animal, the back accompanies the movement, the neck aids in balance, and the hindquarters provide much of the thrust. Everything works together with precision. When the gallop is smooth and regular, one sees a succession of supple and powerful leaps that give the horse a majestic gait.

The gallop is not only beautiful; it is also very useful. In the wild, this gait allowed the horse to flee quickly or cover distance at high speed. For humans, it has become essential in many equestrian disciplines. However, it requires more effort than the walk or trot, as the body works with greater intensity.

Watching a horse gallop is like witnessing a true spectacle of movement. Each stride combines strength, rhythm, and balance with astonishing elegance. It's no wonder this gait has fascinated people for so long. For a few moments, the horse seems to do more than just run. It appears to carry with it the wind, the momentum, and all the energy of the open plain.

Fact 34 - Horses change gaits to conserve energy

A horse doesn't always move the same way, and that's no accident. It often chooses the gait that requires the least effort for the situation at hand. The walk, trot, and gallop aren't just for moving faster or slower. They also help the horse manage its energy more efficiently over the course of a journey.

When the horse moves at a leisurely pace, the walk is often the most economical gait. It allows the horse to walk for a long time without tiring too quickly. If the speed needs to increase, the horse switches to a trot, which becomes more efficient for covering more ground. Then, if urgency or speed demands it, the gallop takes over with much greater power.

Each gait therefore has its own advantage. The walk conserves energy over time, the trot offers a good balance between speed and energy expenditure, and the gallop is used primarily to move quickly over a shorter distance. The horse changes gaits much like we change our pace, shifting between a leisurely walk, a light jog, and a sudden sprint.

The terrain also plays an important role in this choice. Whether on hard ground, a slope, an uneven path, or an open space, the horse adapts the way it moves. It seeks the most practical solution to maintain its balance without wasting energy. Its body does not move randomly; instead, it adjusts its movement with true natural intelligence.

When you see a horse change its gait, you are witnessing a very clever decision made by its entire body. It doesn't change just to look pretty or to impress. It does so to move forward as efficiently as possible, without wasting energy. This is clear proof that, for a horse, power is always accompanied by remarkable efficiency.

Fact 35 - A horse turns quickly thanks to its balance

When a horse turns quickly, it doesn't simply change direction at the last moment. Its entire body works together to maintain stability. Its head, neck, back, and legs work together with precision. This movement looks simple to watch, but it actually requires remarkable coordination to avoid falling and remain fluid.

To execute a turn successfully, the horse shifts its weight with finesse. It adjusts its body position, engages certain limbs more effectively, and uses its neck as a natural counterweight. Its hooves also find their place carefully on the ground. Thanks to this highly precise coordination, it can turn quickly without losing any of its momentum.

Balance plays an essential role here. A horse that turns too abruptly without proper coordination risks slipping or tripping over itself. Its body must therefore calculate the speed, the curve, and the weight distribution on each leg almost simultaneously. It is a true feat of movement, especially for an animal as large, powerful, and fast as a horse.

This ability is very useful in a horse's life. In the wild, it allowed the horse to change direction in case of a surprise or to avoid a sudden obstacle. With humans, it becomes invaluable in many activities, such as arena work or certain equestrian sports. Turning quickly is therefore not only impressive, it is also extremely practical.

When you see a horse execute a quick turn with elegance, you're witnessing a true balancing act. Strength alone wouldn't be enough. What makes this movement possible is the harmony between all parts of its body. Behind this almost instantaneous turn lies an intelligence of movement that makes the horse even more fascinating.

Fact 36 - Foals run shortly after birth

No sooner has it arrived in the world than the foal must already face a huge challenge. In a very short time, it tries to stand up on its long, still-wobbly legs. This speed may seem incredible, yet it is very useful. In horses, foals are born with bodies already ready to move almost immediately after birth.

In the first few hours, the foal first tries to stand up, then to stay upright without falling. It's not easy, as its legs sometimes seem too long for it. It wobbles, slips a little, tries again, and then makes rapid progress. Soon after, it can already walk alongside its mother and even break into a clumsy little trot.

This astonishing speed exists for a good reason. Horses are animals that, in the wild, needed to be able to keep up with the herd without waiting too long. A foal unable to move would be more exposed to danger and risk being separated from its mother— . Knowing how to stand up and run early therefore increases its chances of staying safe.

Even though the foal can run very fast right after birth, that doesn't mean it has already mastered its body perfectly. Its first movements are often hesitant, bounding, and sometimes amusing to watch. Every step teaches it something. In just a few days, it's already gaining balance, coordination, and confidence, almost like a little acrobat in training.

Watching a foal start running so early feels like witnessing a real-life miracle. Just yesterday, it wasn't even there in the pasture, and now here it is, already moving alongside its mother. This feat shows just how remarkably prepared the horse is from the very start of its life, with astonishing energy and a strong will to move forward.

Fact 37 - The horse jumps by coordinating its entire body

When a horse jumps, it doesn't just push hard with its legs. Its entire body works together in a very precise sequence. The head, neck, back, shoulders, belly, and limbs all participate in the movement. It is therefore not a simple leap. It is a true coordination of the body, almost like a perfectly choreographed dance.

Before the obstacle, the horse is already preparing for its jump. It adjusts its speed, measures the distance, and places its strides carefully. Then it lowers its hindquarters slightly to build up power. At the right moment, it pushes strongly with its hind legs. This thrust propels it forward and upward with impressive and highly controlled energy.

During the jump, the neck plays a major role in maintaining balance. It stretches forward to support the movement, while the back rises and the forelimbs bend. The horse then guides its body over the obstacle with precision. Every part must come together at the right moment. Otherwise, the jump becomes less fluid, less comfortable, and far less effective.

After clearing the obstacle, the work is not done. The horse must still land without losing its composure. It lands first on its forelimbs, then its hindlimbs, all while regaining its balance to set off again. This landing requires just as much coordination as the takeoff. The body must absorb the impact, maintain the axis of movement, and remain ready for the next stride.

Watching a horse jump is about admiring much more than a spectacular leap. It is observing an animal capable of combining strength, flexibility, precision, and timing in a single movement. Behind every cleared obstacle lies incredible teamwork among all parts of the body. The jump thus reveals the full intelligence of the horse's movement, elegant and powerful at the same time.

Fact 38 - Some horses are famous for their endurance

Not all horses shine in the same way. Some impress with their speed, others with their strength, and a few are especially admired for their endurance. This means they can cover long distances while maintaining their energy for a long time. This quality is so remarkable that it has given rise to a special discipline called equestrian endurance.

In this discipline, the goal isn't just to go fast. The horse must also stay in shape throughout the course, sometimes over very long distances. Endurance competitions therefore test the rider's speed, stamina, and ability to manage their effort. It's a true test of endurance.

Among the horses best known for this quality, the Arabian horse holds a special place. Organizations specializing in this breed explain that it is famous for its great endurance, stamina, and ability to perform well over long distances. In many events, Arabian horses are often among the top performers.

This reputation is no accident. To succeed in endurance riding, a horse must combine good physical condition, a calm temperament, and a great ability to conserve energy. It's not enough to be brave for just a few minutes. You have to last, stay consistent, and keep moving forward intelligently throughout the entire course. It's a truly unique talent.

When we talk about horses famous for their endurance, we're thinking of true champions of stamina. They aren't just after a quick feat. They show that a horse can be powerful, brave, and patient all at once. Their talent reminds us of a valuable lesson: moving forward for a long time with wisdom can be just as impressive as a lightning-fast start.

Fact 39 - The Back Muscles Work With Every Stride

When a horse moves forward, we often look at its legs, as they seem to do all the work. Yet its back is also involved in every movement. With every stride, the muscles running along its spine contract, relax, and then start over. Without them, the horse would have a much harder time staying supple, balanced, and powerful while moving.

The back does more than just connect the front and back of the body. It also transmits the energy generated by the hind legs to the rest of the horse. When the hindquarters push, the back supports this movement and helps the entire body move forward in harmony. It's a bit like a living bridge—strong yet flexible—that works constantly.

Whether walking, trotting, or galloping, these muscles never function exactly the same way. They adapt to the gait, the speed, and even the terrain. On a flat path, they stabilize the movement. On an incline or during a jump, they exert even more effort. Each stride thus becomes a delicate balance between strength and suppleness.

A healthy back is very important for a horse's comfort. If it is stiff, tired, or overused, the horse's movements become less fluid and its entire body can be affected. That is why care, appropriate exercise, and good posture are so important. A horse that uses its back properly often moves with greater ease.

When you see a horse moving with elegance, think of all those invisible muscles working beneath its skin. Its back is never passive, even when everything looks effortless. It supports, transmits, balances, and accompanies every step. This subtle detail reveals yet another fascinating truth: in horses, power always comes from the beautiful cooperation of the entire body.

Fact 40 - Horses know how to adapt their stride to the terrain

A horse does not place its hooves the same way everywhere. On grass, mud, gravel, or hard ground, it naturally changes the way it moves. It adjusts the length of its strides, its speed, and sometimes even its posture. This ability helps it stay stable and avoid wasting energy unnecessarily.

On slippery ground, for example, the horse often becomes more cautious. It shortens its strides, places its feet more carefully, and moves forward with greater attention. On uneven ground, it pays closer attention to where it places its hooves. Its body then functions like a true tightrope walker. Each step is chosen carefully to minimize risks and maintain good stability.

When the terrain slopes up or down, the horse also adapts its movement. On an uphill slope, it pushes harder with its hindquarters to move forward. On a downhill slope, it often slows down and better manages its balance so as not to be carried away. Its neck, back, and legs then work together precisely to help it navigate the terrain without losing its composure.

This ability stems from its experience, its sense of balance, and its awareness of the ground. The horse quickly senses whether the ground is firm, soft, uneven, or unstable. It doesn't think in words, of course, but its body quickly understands what needs to be done. It is a subtle, natural, and very impressive intelligence of movement.

Watching a horse move across different terrains is to see an animal that adjusts its movements with great finesse. It doesn't just walk forward. It reads the ground, anticipates difficulties, and modifies its movement at the right moment. This is yet another remarkable talent of the horse, capable of combining caution, suppleness, and elegance with every stride.

Chapter 5 : Nutrition and Digestion

Fact 41 - Horses Eat Almost All Day Long

In the wild, horses do not eat three large meals like many humans. They eat slowly, in small amounts, over many hours. Their bodies are designed to receive a nearly constant supply of fiber from grass. That is why a horse in a pasture often spends much of its day with its head down, quietly grazing.

This behavior isn't gluttony. It's a very useful habit for their digestion. A horse's stomach is quite small relative to its size, so it works best when food arrives regularly. Eating often also helps keep its mind occupied and maintain its natural rhythm. For a horse, grazing for long periods is a normal and important activity.

When a horse lives in a pasture, it moves forward as it eats. It takes a bite, takes a few steps, then starts over again and again. This slow movement allows it to seek out the best grasses while remaining attentive to its surroundings. Even during these quiet moments, it continues to observe, listen, and live in tune with the herd.

Hay often plays a similar role when grass is scarce or when the horse lives in a different setting. It, too, provides fiber that the horse chews for a long time. This prolonged chewing is valuable because it supports the work of its digestive system. A horse that can eat regularly often feels calmer and more comfortable.

The next time you see a horse grazing for hours, you'll know it's not just taking an endless meal break. It's actually following a very ancient rhythm of life, perfectly suited to its body. For the horse, eating for long periods is part of its balance, almost like walking, breathing, or spending time with other horses.

Fact 42 - Grass is the favorite food of many horses

When we picture a horse in a pasture, we often see it with its head bent toward the ground, grazing calmly. This image is very accurate, because grass is one of its most natural foods. For a very long time, horses have been designed to forage for food in wide-open spaces. Their bodies and teeth are perfectly adapted to this habit.

Grass primarily provides them with fiber, which is very important for their digestion. Horses do not eat quickly. They cut the grass with their front teeth, then chew it thoroughly with their molars. This patient chewing helps their bodies function properly. That is why they often prefer to eat little by little over many hours rather than gulp down a large meal all at once.

Not all grasses are alike, and horses often know how to choose the ones they prefer. They may graze certain parts of the pasture with more enthusiasm than others. Their noses, lips, and experience help them identify what suits them best. It is therefore not just a matter of hunger, but also of careful selection.

Grass fits well with their natural rhythm of life. As it grazes, the horse moves slowly, observes its surroundings, and often stays close to others. It eats while continuing to monitor its environment. This calm activity takes up a large part of its day and contributes to its balance. For the horse, feeding and moving often go hand in hand.

Watching a horse graze is therefore far from ordinary once you understand what is really happening. It follows an ancient way of life, perfectly attuned to its body. Grass is not just another food. For many horses, it is an ideal, simple, and precious food that supports their health, calmness, and natural way of life.

Fact 43 - Horses need meals spread out throughout the day

A horse's stomach does not function like that of a human who eats a few large meals a day. Its digestive system is designed to receive small amounts of food very regularly. In the wild, it grazes for long periods, almost without hurrying. Its body therefore prefers a continuous supply rather than a large quantity swallowed all at once.

A horse's stomach is quite small for an animal of its size. It cannot store a large amount of food at once without discomfort. On the other hand, its intestines are very large to digest the fiber from grass and hay. Its entire system is therefore designed for a slow, steady, and patient rhythm, perfectly suited to grazing.

When meals are well-spaced, digestion generally proceeds more smoothly. The horse chews for a long time, produces more saliva, and gradually sends the food into its digestive system. This respects its natural functioning. Conversely, large meals spaced too far apart do not really align with the way its body was designed to work.

This regular rhythm also helps the horse stay more calm. Eating frequently takes up a significant part of its day and aligns with its deep-rooted habits. A horse that can nibble on hay or graze at appropriate intervals finds it easier to maintain a balanced daily routine. For horses, a comfortable stomach and overall calmness often go hand in hand.

Understanding this allows us to see the horse in a different light. This large, powerful animal actually has a rather delicate digestive system that prefers regularity over excess. Its meals should follow a gentle rhythm, almost like a melody repeated throughout the day. Here is yet another example of how, with horses, patience is often the best ally.

Fact 44 - Horses drink more than you might think

No matter how much grass or hay a horse eats, it also needs plenty of water every day. This large, powerful body cannot function properly without proper hydration. Drinking helps with digestion, transports nutrients, and keeps the body in shape. For horses, water is therefore almost as important as food.

The amount a horse drinks depends on its size, the heat, its activity level, and what it eats. A horse that is working, sweating, or spending time outdoors on a hot day will naturally need to drink more. Even a horse at rest needs water regularly. Its body is constantly using up its water reserves, even when it appears calm in the pasture.

Hay, for example, contains much less water than fresh grass. A horse fed mainly on hay therefore often needs to drink even more to compensate. When it grazes on green, moist grass, part of its water intake already comes from its food. Its needs therefore vary depending on the seasons, living conditions, and the type of feed it receives.

Drinking also helps the horse after exertion. When it has galloped, trotted for a long time, or been out in the hot sun, its body loses water through sweating. It must then replenish its reserves to restore balance. A well-hydrated horse generally feels better, digests food more efficiently, and recovers more easily. Water is therefore essential for all of the body's major functions.

The next time you see a horse drinking for a long time, you'll know it's not just taking a quick break. It's fulfilling an essential need of its body. Behind this simple act lies a true vital necessity. For this impressive animal, water is a silent ally, indispensable for moving forward, digesting, recovering, and staying in top shape.

Fact 45 - A horse's teeth wear down by grinding fiber

A horse's teeth work extremely hard every day. Unlike us, it spends long hours chewing grass or hay, foods rich in fiber. This prolonged work naturally wears down its teeth. This isn't an unusual problem; in fact, it's intended by nature. For a horse, eating slowly is part of the body's normal functioning.

When a horse grazes, it first cuts the grass with its front teeth. Then, its large back teeth, called molars, grind the food with rhythmic movements. These movements constantly rub against the tooth surfaces. As the horse repeats this action for hours on end, the teeth gradually wear down, much like a file that works nonstop.

This natural wear is important because a horse's teeth grow throughout most of its life. This growth compensates for the friction caused by chewing. It's a very clever system. Without this gradual growth, the teeth would become too short. The horse is therefore equipped to wear down its teeth while continuing to chew effectively over the years.

But sometimes, the wear doesn't happen perfectly evenly. Certain areas can become too sharp or wear down differently depending on how the horse chews. This can make it difficult for the horse to eat comfortably. That's why we monitor its teeth closely. A healthy mouth helps it grind down the fibers properly and enjoy its meals to the fullest.

The next time you see a horse chewing its hay for a long time, think about this incredible natural machine hidden in its mouth. Every bite puts its teeth to work with patience and precision. This unassuming detail reveals something essential: for a horse, even the simple act of eating is a meticulous, ingenious activity perfectly adapted to its life.

Fact 46 - Hay helps horses digest properly in winter

When winter arrives, grass in pastures often becomes scarcer, shorter, or less nutritious. Hay then plays a very important role in a horse's diet. It's not just a substitute. It's a valuable food, made from cut and dried grass, that helps the horse continue to eat at its natural pace.

A horse's digestive system thrives on fiber, and hay provides plenty of it. By chewing it slowly, the horse also produces a lot of saliva, which aids the digestive process. Since horses eat slowly and frequently, hay is well-suited to their needs. It helps their digestive system function regularly, even when winter disrupts their routine.

Hay also helps the horse stay occupied longer on cold days. In the wild, it would spend a large portion of its time searching for and eating grass. In winter, hay allows it to maintain this more regular rhythm. This detail matters a great deal, as the horse generally feels better when its diet aligns with its usual functioning.

A horse that receives good hay can therefore continue to chew, digest, and move more comfortably during the cold season. The fiber nourishes its body effectively and helps it use its energy efficiently. Since chewing takes time, it also prevents the horse from eating too quickly. Despite its simple appearance, hay thus provides great benefits every winter day.

When you see a horse burying its nose in a pile of hay on a cold day, you're witnessing much more than just a meal. You're seeing a food perfectly suited to its body and the season. Thanks to hay, the horse regains a reassuring rhythm, more regular digestion, and a natural way to get through the winter with calm and comfort.

Fact 47 - A horse doesn't eat like a cow

You might think that all large grazing animals eat the same way, but that's not true. Horses and cows don't use the same digestive system at all. Both love grass, yet the way they process it is very different. Their meals look similar from the outside, but on the inside, the work going on is truly not the same.

Cows are ruminants. This means they have a very unique digestive system with several compartments in their stomach. They first swallow the grass quickly, then bring it back up into their mouth to chew it again. This second pass is called rumination. Horses, on the other hand, never ruminate. Once swallowed, the food simply continues on its way.

In horses, the stomach is much smaller than a cow's. Their bodies are designed to receive small amounts of food over long periods of time. They must therefore eat slowly and frequently. Fiber digestion occurs primarily further down the digestive tract, in a highly developed section of the intestine. This is another strategy—discreet but highly effective.

This difference also changes how these animals are fed. A cow can handle its meals differently than a horse, because its body doesn't have the same habits. The horse, on the other hand, does better with food spread out throughout the day. Its body likes regularity. It prefers to graze for a long time rather than have a few very large meals.

The next time you see a horse grazing in a field, don't imagine it eating like a nearby cow. Even if the grass is the same, the journey through the digestive tract is very different. This comparison reveals something fascinating: nature devises multiple solutions to process the same food, and each is perfectly adapted to the animal that possesses it.

Fact 48 - Horses Need Salt and Minerals

Horses don't live on just grass, hay, and water. Their bodies also need small but very important substances, such as salt and minerals. Even in very small amounts, they help many parts of the body function properly. Without them, muscles, nerves, bones, and many other systems would work much less efficiently.

Salt, for example, mainly provides sodium and chloride. These elements help the body maintain proper water balance and ensure that certain messages are transmitted effectively throughout the body. When a horse sweats, it loses some of this salt. That's why its needs may increase when it's hot or when the horse is exerting itself.

As for minerals, there are many, and each has its own role. Calcium and phosphorus contribute to the strength of bones and teeth. Magnesium helps muscles function properly. Other minerals play a part in small, invisible but essential tasks. The horse's body is therefore like a large team where each of these elements has a specific mission.

In daily life, horses get some of these elements from their diet. Grass, hay, and other foods already contain them. However, this isn't always enough, depending on the situation. That's why a salt block is often placed near them. The horse can then come and lick it when its body feels the need.

This story shows that a large, powerful animal also depends on tiny things we hardly ever notice. A little salt, a few minerals, and the whole body can function better. Behind its hooves, mane, and strength, the horse thus hides a very precise mechanism. Even the smallest elements matter in keeping such a beautiful animal going.

Fact 49 - A poor diet disrupts the horse

Horses have powerful bodies, but their balance is quite delicate. Their digestive health, muscles, energy levels, and even their temperament depend heavily on what they eat each day. If their diet does not meet their actual needs, various problems can arise. For horses, therefore, feeding is not just a minor detail. It is an essential foundation for the entire body.

Its digestive system prefers small, well-spaced meals rich in fiber, such as grass or hay. If food is introduced improperly, too quickly, or in excessive quantities, the body can be disrupted. The horse may then become less comfortable, less calm, or less fit. Its system thrives on consistency, not sudden changes.

An unsuitable diet can also affect its movements. A poorly nourished horse may lack energy, lose comfort, or show increased tension. Its muscles work less efficiently, recovery becomes more difficult, and its behavior may change. Even though it cannot speak, its body sends signals. It shows that something in its balance is not right.

The quality of the food matters just as much as the quantity. Overly rich grass, poor-quality hay, or poorly organized meals do not yield the same results as a simple, appropriate diet. The horse needs water, fiber, minerals, and a stable routine. Its body functions better when each element is in its proper place.

Understanding this allows us to see the horse in a different light. This large, elegant animal depends on a very precise balance between what it eats, what it drinks, and how its meals are distributed. When its diet suits it, it often feels more serene and more responsive. Feeding a horse well, therefore, is already taking care of everything it is.

Fact 50 - Grazing slowly follows the horse's rhythm

In a pasture, a horse often spends long hours grazing without rushing. It moves slowly, takes a bite, takes a few steps, then starts over. This behavior may seem very simple, but it actually follows the natural rhythm of its body. A horse is not built to eat quickly. It is designed to feed slowly and almost continuously.

This way of eating suits its digestive system perfectly. Its stomach is quite small, so it prefers to receive small, regular amounts rather than one very large meal. By grazing slowly, it chews for a long time, produces saliva, and helps its stomach work properly. This leisurely pace is therefore a real help in keeping its body comfortable.

Grazing slowly also helps the horse stay calm. While eating, it continues to observe its surroundings, listen for sounds, and track the movements of other horses. It isn't just having a meal. It is living, staying alert, and moving at its own pace. For a horse, eating and staying attentive to the world often happen at the same time.

This natural rhythm corresponds to the life horses have led for thousands of years in wide-open spaces. They had to search for food while constantly moving forward, all the while keeping an eye on their surroundings. Slow grazing is therefore not a lazy habit. It is a very intelligent way to eat, move, and stay ready to react.

When you see a horse grazing calmly for a long time, you're observing much more than just a simple mealtime. You're seeing an animal following the deep rhythm of its nature. Every bite, every step, and every pause speak to this ancient harmony between its body and its way of life. In horses, slowness can be a true form of intelligence.

Chapter 6 : Wild Life and Adaptation

Fact 51 - Horses often live in groups for safety

Horses often feel safer when surrounded by other horses. In the wild, staying in a group allows them to spot dangers more easily and react more quickly. While some graze peacefully, others keep watch. This shared vigilance makes life safer and explains why horses often seek the company of their own kind.

When several horses live together, each benefits from the eyes, ears, and reactions of the others. If one of them suddenly raises its head, stretches its neck, or freezes, the others understand that they need to be on guard. This system is very effective, as an entire herd can become alert in a matter of seconds, sometimes even before everyone has seen the cause.

Living in a group also helps horses stay calmer. Being alone can make a horse more anxious, as it must monitor the entire area without help. With companions, this burden is shared. The herd then acts somewhat like a large, silent team, where each member contributes their presence, their observation, and their way of reacting to changes.

Young horses learn a great deal from this communal life. They observe the adults, discover the group's rules, and understand how to maintain proper distances. They also learn when to follow, when to wait, and when to remain cautious. The herd, therefore, serves not only to protect itself. It also becomes a living school where they learn to live together harmoniously.

When you see horses gathered in a field, you're not just looking at a group sharing the same space. You're witnessing an ancient, highly intelligent strategy crafted by nature. By staying together, horses gain safety, calm, and experience. Their group life shows that together, we can often observe better and feel stronger.

Fact 52 - In the wild, horses move every day

In the wild, a horse doesn't stay in one place for long. It moves steadily to find grass, water, a quieter spot, or better shelter. Its way of life is therefore tied to movement. Walking has been part of its daily routine for thousands of years, almost as much as eating, drinking, or staying with other horses.

These movements aren't like a nonstop sprint. Most often, horses walk calmly over long distances, grazing as they go. They move forward, stop, observe, then set off again a little further on. This slow but steady pace allows them to explore their surroundings without wasting energy. Their day unfolds this way, step by step.

Moving frequently is very beneficial for their bodies. Walking helps the muscles work gently, maintains the hooves, and aids digestion. A horse is built to move steadily, not to remain motionless for long hours. Its legs, back, and abdomen function better when movement is part of its daily life.

These journeys also serve the group's safety. By moving together, horses can seek out the best areas to eat while keeping an eye on their surroundings. They avoid less suitable spots, sometimes follow the same paths, and get to know their territory. This memory of places helps them move with confidence and stay calmer.

When you imagine a wild horse, don't just picture it galloping in a huge cloud of dust. Think also of all those miles traveled quietly each day. Its true strength is shown not only in speed, but also in its ability to move for long distances, with calm, endurance, and an astonishing fidelity to nature's rhythm.

Fact 53 - Horses perceive danger better in the open air

Horses often feel more at ease in open spaces than in enclosed areas. This is no coincidence. On plains, meadows, or large open fields, they can fully utilize their wide- . They spot movements in the distance more easily and have more time to understand what is happening around them.

Their eyes, positioned on the sides of their heads, provide a wide field of vision. In an open space, this advantage becomes even more useful. Horses can monitor multiple directions at once without moving much. A distant figure, an animal crossing the path, or a detail moving in the grass quickly catches their attention and helps them stay alert.

Narrow spaces, on the other hand, provide less information at a glance. Walls, dense hedges, or enclosed passages limit its vision and can make it more hesitant. It sees less far ahead, anticipates less effectively, and may feel less secure. For an animal that likes to observe before acting, this lack of visual space matters greatly.

In the wild, this preference served an important purpose. A horse living in open areas could better spot changes around it and move away quickly if necessary. It wasn't just looking for grass. It was also looking for places where its vision and speed could work together. The landscape then gave it a real advantage.

When you see a horse raise its head in a wide-open field and scan the horizon, you're witnessing a scene that comes naturally to it. It's making the most of its sentinel's gaze. Open spaces allow it to see sooner, understand faster, and feel safer. That's why the vast plain seems to suit it so well.

Fact 54 - Horse coats follow surprising rules

A horse's coat refers to the color of its hair, but also that of its mane, tail, and sometimes its skin. At first glance, all of this seems very varied and a bit mysterious. However, these differences are not chosen at random. They depend on natural rules related to heredity—that is, what the parents pass on to the foal.

Some coat colors are very well known, such as bay, where the body is brown with a black mane and extremities, or chestnut, where the hair has a reddish tint. There are also black, gray, and many other shades. Sometimes white markings on the head or legs are added to this, making each horse even more recognizable.

Behind these colors lie invisible genetic instructions within the horse's body. These rules govern the production of pigments—the substances that give the hair its color. Depending on the combinations inherited from its parents, a foal may be born with a specific coat color. It's a bit like a secret recipe where each ingredient slightly alters the final result.

Some coats even hold surprises. The gray horse, for example, may be born dark and then gradually lighten as it grows. Other horses have distinctive markings, such as spots or large white patches, according to very specific hereditary rules. Nature, therefore, does not paint horses at random. It follows precise mechanisms, sometimes simple, sometimes much more surprising.

When you look at a horse, its coat already tells a small part of its story. It speaks of its family, of what it received at birth, and sometimes of changes that will appear over time. Beneath their magnificent colors, horses thus hide a real lesson in science. Their beauty also stems from remarkably well-organized natural rules.

Fact 55 - Some horses tolerate the cold very well

Not all horses react the same way to winter. Some tolerate low temperatures very well thanks to several natural defenses. As the days grow colder, their bodies gradually prepare. Their coat thickens, their skin functions differently, and their bodies adapt to better retain heat without unnecessary effort.

Their winter coat plays a very important role. The hairs stand up slightly and trap a layer of air close to the body. This air acts somewhat like an insulating blanket. If the horse stays dry and can shelter from the wind, this protection becomes very effective. Under this seasonal coat, body heat escapes much more slowly.

Horses also generate heat by eating, especially when they chew hay for a long time. Digesting fiber requires work from their bodies, and this work helps maintain their temperature. It's a kind of internal heating system—discreet but invaluable. That's why an appropriate diet is particularly important during the cold and wet times of the year.

Certain breeds from regions with harsh climates are even better equipped. They often have very dense coats, tough skin, and a build well-suited to harsh seasons. That doesn't mean they don't need anything. Even a cold-hardy horse must have access to water, a sheltered spot, and good living conditions.

When you see a calm horse in a pasture in winter, it isn't necessarily shivering beneath its thick coat. Its body sometimes knows exactly how to handle the cold. This ability once again demonstrates nature's ingenuity. Beneath its tranquil appearance, the horse hides a true knack for weathering the seasons with courage and efficiency.

Fact 56 - Some horses live in hot, dry climates

Not all horses live in the same landscapes. Some are particularly well-adapted to hot, dry, and sometimes dusty regions. In these environments, they must endure the sun, walk long distances, and find sustenance in a less bountiful natural world. Over time, certain horses have developed qualities that are very useful for coping with this type of climate.

Their bodies often display great simplicity. Many have a slender build, sturdy limbs, and a good ability to cover long distances without tiring too quickly. They know how to conserve their energy and move with steady rhythm. In regions where water and grass may be scarce, this endurance becomes a highly valuable asset.

The Arabian horse is one of the best-known examples of this adaptation. Bred for a very long time in arid areas, it is famous for its resilience, energy, and staying power. Its physique, stamina, and temperament enable it to cope with demanding conditions and . It demonstrates just how perfectly a horse can be attuned to its environment.

In hot regions, it's not just about running fast. You also have to know how to manage the heat, move forward on sometimes difficult terrain, and remain effective despite a taxing climate. These adapted horses often cope better with these conditions thanks to their experience, their hardiness, and the traits passed down through generations by their lineage.

When we think of horses, we sometimes imagine only green plains or damp meadows. Yet some thrive and excel in much drier lands. Their presence reminds us of a fascinating truth: nature knows how to shape animals capable of adapting to very different worlds. The horse does not merely conquer space; it also learns to adapt to the climate.

Fact 57 - Hooves change depending on the ground and activity

A horse's hoof appears very hard, almost like a material that never changes. Yet it evolves over time depending on where the horse walks and what it does each day. A horse living on dry, stony, or wet ground does not wear down its hooves in the same way. Its foot therefore gradually adapts to these conditions.

On hard ground, the hoof may wear down more, as each step rubs more forcefully against the ground. On softer ground, such as grass or soft soil, the wear is often different. The hoof grows continuously, then balances out what it loses. It's a bit like the horse's foot slowly reshaping itself according to its daily life.

The horse's activity also plays an important role. A horse that walks a lot on varied terrain does not put as much strain on its hooves as a horse that moves little. An animal that works, trots, gallops, or turns frequently uses its feet more intensely. The hoof must then withstand greater stress and adapt to more demanding movements.

This ability to adapt is very useful, because the hoof is not just a hard shell. It is a living part of the body that grows, wears down, and responds to the stresses of daily life. That is why hoof care is so important. Observing the hooves helps you understand how the horse lives, moves, and uses its body on different terrains.

When you look at a horse's hooves, you see much more than just four points of contact at the ends of its legs. You see living structures that tell the story of its lifestyle, its efforts, and the ground it walks on. Beneath their simple appearance, hooves reveal an incredible capacity for adaptation. In horses, even the feet know how to intelligently adjust to the outside world.

Fact 58 - Horses turn into the wind to escape insects

In summer, insects can become very bothersome for horses. Flies, horseflies, and other small pests buzz around their eyes, necks, or flanks. At such times, many horses prefer spots where the air circulates well. The wind isn't just pleasant; it also helps them get rid of some of these annoying invaders.

When a breeze blows, insects have a harder time flying close to the horse's body or landing quietly on its skin. The wind disrupts their flight path and sometimes prevents them from approaching certain sensitive areas. That's why a horse might choose a spot that's more exposed to the air rather than a place that's calm but stuffy and full of insects.

This behavior is often observed in pastures. Horses position themselves on higher ground, near an opening, or in an open space where the air circulates better. They may also turn their bodies to face the direction of the wind. This choice is no accident. It's a very practical way to use the environment to find a little more comfort.

Of course, the wind isn't their only defense. The tail swats away flies, the mane protects part of the neck, and the skin quivers to scare off certain insects. Still, seeking out the breeze remains a very useful strategy. Horses thus combine several simple, natural, and effective methods to better endure days when insects are plentiful.

The next time you see a horse standing still in the wind, it might not just be daydreaming. It's likely taking advantage of some invisible help from above. This habit shows once again just how well horses observe their environment and use it intelligently. Even a simple breeze can become a valuable ally for them.

Fact 59 - A herd is calmer if it knows its surroundings

Horses like to know where they live. When a herd is familiar with its pasture, paths, shelters, and the usual sounds of the area, it often remains more relaxed. The animals know where to find water, where to rest, and where to move about. This familiarity reduces surprises and helps each horse feel safer in everyday life.

In a familiar place, horses can easily tell what's normal and what isn't. A tree, a fence, a gate, or a path is already part of their memory. If something new appears, they can spot it faster. Since the rest of the surroundings are familiar, they don't need to monitor everything with the same intensity.

This familiarity with the location also aids relationships within the herd. Horses have a better sense of where to position themselves, how to pass one another, and which spots are convenient for eating or resting. Movement becomes more fluid, and there is often less hesitation. The group then functions with greater consistency, almost as if following a well-learned invisible map.

Conversely, a new environment can make horses more alert and sometimes more nervous. They observe more, test the surroundings, and look for their bearings. This behavior is normal. Calm often returns as they gradually memorize the smells, paths, objects, and routines of the place. Their confidence grows as the place becomes familiar.

When you see a peaceful herd in a pasture they know well, you're witnessing more than just a moment of rest. You're seeing horses settled into a world they understand. This familiarity with their surroundings helps them live together with greater peace of mind. For them, calm often stems from a very simple secret: knowing where they are and recognizing what's around them.

Fact 60 - Horses find passable paths

When a horse moves through varied terrain, it doesn't walk randomly. It observes the ground, senses its stability under its hooves, and often chooses the easiest spot to pass. Between rocks, a slope, or a muddy area, it naturally seeks the most passable route. Its entire body seems to think with astonishing precision.

This ability stems from several qualities working together. The horse possesses a good sense of balance, keen attention to the terrain, and a useful memory of paths already taken. Its eyes scan the terrain, its legs test the ground, and its hooves quickly sense whether the ground is firm or slippery. Each step thus provides valuable information.

On a difficult path, it sometimes shortens its strides, slightly changes direction, or slows down to place its feet more carefully. On a slope, it positions its body differently than on flat ground. On rocky terrain, it seeks out the most stable areas. This is not unnecessary hesitation. It is an intelligent way to avoid missteps.

Humans have long noticed this skill. An experienced horse often knows the comfortable paths better than we imagine, especially on natural terrain. It can go around a deep puddle, avoid an area that's too soft, or choose a safer curve. Its caution isn't laziness. On the contrary, it shows an excellent reading of the terrain.

When you see a horse moving calmly over difficult terrain, watch closely where it places its hooves. You'll discover a true expert on trails. Without a map, sign, or words, it often finds the best path forward. This quiet talent reminds us that the horse isn't just fast and strong. It's also a remarkable explorer of the ground.

Chapter 7 : History and Great Discoveries

Fact 61 - Humans domesticated horses long ago

A very long time ago, humans lived surrounded by wild animals, and the horse was one of them. Then, over the centuries, certain groups began to keep them, feed them, and have them live near them. Researchers believe this domestication dates back to about 5,500 to 6,000 years ago, primarily in the vast steppes of Eurasia.

For a long time, scientists have been very interested in a site called Botai, in present-day Kazakhstan. Very ancient evidence related to horses has been found there, dating back to around 3500 BCE. These discoveries showed that humans were already caring for horses very early on, even though the exact history of the first domesticated horses remains a subject of debate.

Domesticating a horse did not simply mean taming it a little. It meant raising it, using it, and passing this practice down from generation to generation. Little by little, the horse changed human life. It helped people move faster, carry loads, and, later, travel farther than before. Its arrival transformed many societies.

The story is even more fascinating because recent studies show that modern domestic horses appear to originate primarily from the steppes of western Eurasia, particularly the Volga-Don region. This means that several significant stages likely occurred before today's domestic horse became widely distributed across the globe.

When you see a peaceful horse in a meadow, it's hard to imagine that its history with humans began millennia ago. Yet this ancient bond has changed the fate of both. The horse wasn't just domesticated. It became an essential companion on humanity's journey through time.

Fact 62 - The horse revolutionized long-distance travel

Before the advent of trains, cars, and airplanes, traveling long distances required a great deal of time and effort. On foot, humans moved slowly and could carry very little. The use of the horse changed everything. Thanks to the horse, it became possible to cover much greater distances in a single day and to reach places that were once difficult to access.

Horses weren't just used to go faster. They also made it possible to carry bags, tools, provisions, and sometimes very important messages. On roads, trails, and plains, they became true travel companions. Their endurance, strength, and ability to travel long distances opened up the world to many travelers.

Merchants, messengers, explorers, and ordinary travelers relied on them for centuries. With horses, news traveled faster between cities, markets were better connected, and certain journeys over long distances finally became possible. Thus, the horse helped move not only people, but also ideas, objects, and information.

On certain routes, relay stations were set up to change horses and continue the journey without losing too much time. This system made travel even more efficient. It demonstrated just how indispensable the horse had become in many regions. Without it, crossing vast territories would have been much slower, more tiring, and far more complicated.

When we think of the great journeys of the past, we must imagine the sound of hooves on the paths and the silhouette of the horse patiently advancing toward the horizon. It did not merely transport humans. It brought cities, peoples, and distant horizons closer together. Thanks to it, the world suddenly seemed a little less vast and much more accessible.

Fact 63 - Horses have long helped plow the fields

For centuries, the horse has been an invaluable helper in agricultural work. Long before tractors, it helped human farmers turn the soil to prepare the fields for crops. Harnessed to a plow, it moved forward with strength and steady rhythm. Thanks to the horse, fields could be worked more quickly than by human muscle alone.

Plowing a field requires a great deal of energy. A heavy implement must be pulled through the soil, sometimes along long, straight lines. The horse was particularly well-suited for this task, as it combined strength, endurance, and obedience. With a good harness and an experienced farmer, it could accomplish a great deal of work throughout the day.

Not all horses were chosen for this role. Certain breeds, which were more robust and massive, were particularly valued for field work. They are often called draft horses. Their powerful bodies, sturdy limbs, and calm temperament made them well-suited for this patient, repetitive, and often demanding work on varied terrain.

Horses weren't just used for plowing. They could also pull carts, transport crops, or assist with other farm tasks. In many rural areas, they were truly part of daily life. Their help saved time, increased the area that could be worked, and made certain tasks less exhausting for humans.

When we imagine the fields of yesteryear, we must picture the slow sound of the plow, the earth being turned, and the horse moving forward with determination. For a long time, its role was essential to feeding villages and towns. Behind many ancient harvests, there was often a patient, sturdy, and incredibly useful horse.

Fact 64 - Messengers used horses to travel

Before the telegraph, the telephone, and computers, delivering urgent news was a real feat. Messengers had to carry letters, orders, or information from one town to another as quickly as possible. To do this, they often relied on horses. Thanks to them, messages traveled much faster than on foot along the roads of yesteryear.

Horses allowed messengers to travel for long hours with great efficiency. On the trails, they could trot , or gallop depending on the urgency and the terrain. Their speed changed everything. Important information arrived sooner, which could help a city, a leader, or an army make a decision at the right moment.

In some countries, relay stations were even set up. The messenger would stop at a station, dismount from his tired horse, and set off almost immediately on a fresh one. This system saved precious time. News could thus travel great distances much faster, almost like a living chain of speed and endurance.

These journeys were not always easy. Messengers had to traverse muddy paths, steep slopes, rivers, or very long roads. They also had to be skilled riders and know how to care for their mounts. The horse was therefore not merely a means of transportation. It became a true partner—courageous, reliable, and indispensable on the most urgent missions.

When we imagine a messenger setting out on the road, we often first picture the letter he is carrying. Yet without his horse, that message would have arrived much later. For centuries, hooves carried vital news across regions. The horse thus played a quiet but immense role in the speed of human communication.

Fact 65 - Some peoples bred warhorses

For a very long period in history, the horse was not used solely for travel or work in the fields. In many civilizations, it also held an important place in the military. Peoples selected, bred, and trained specific horses for combat, as these animals had to be brave, fast, enduring, and capable of obeying commands amid great turmoil.

Not all horses were suited for this role. To pull a chariot, carry a rider, or advance in battle, specific qualities were required. Some societies therefore developed dedicated military breeding programs. In ancient times, war chariots became so important that horse breeding was considered essential to the power of the state.

Other peoples sought horses capable of carrying heavily armed warriors, while some preferred more spirited and maneuverable mounts. Among the Parthians, for example, horses were bred for different purposes depending on the type of combatant. The desired qualities might therefore vary, but the goal remained the same: to train the horse to be as useful as possible for war.

Some regions even became famous for their warhorses. The Urartians, for example, had a reputation for breeding excellent horses specifically for combat. This shows just how important these animals were to military strategy. A good horse could provide greater speed, greater mobility, and sometimes a decisive advantage on the battlefield.

When we think of ancient armies, we often picture weapons or armor. Yet behind many victories and long marches, there were also carefully selected and bred horses. Their presence shaped the history of many civilizations. It reminds us that in the past, a people's strength was sometimes also measured by the quality of their mounts.

Fact 66 - Horses made it possible to connect cities far apart

In the past, traveling from one city to another took a long time. The roads were long, sometimes muddy, and walking didn't allow for much speed. The horse changed that dramatically. Thanks to its speed and endurance, it became a living link between distant places, even when the paths were difficult.

With a horse, a traveler could cover much greater distances in a single day than on foot. Merchants transported their goods, messengers brought news, and travelers reached other regions. Gradually, certain towns that had once been isolated became better connected. Horses didn't just move people; they carried objects, ideas, and information.

In many countries, roads and staging posts were even established to facilitate these journeys. Travelers could change horses, rest for a while, and then set off again quickly. This system made travel more efficient. Thanks to these well-placed stops, important messages traveled great distances with surprising speed for the time.

Horses also facilitated trade between the countryside and cities. They pulled carts, carried bags, accompanied merchants, and connected markets. Thanks to them, goods from one place could reach another more easily. Entire regions grew closer to one another, simply because hooves kept moving forward day after day.

When we think of the great cities of the past, we must imagine the roads that connected them and the horses that traveled them tirelessly. They served as true bridges between worlds that were sometimes very far apart. Without them, much trade would have been much slower. The horse thus bridged distances long before the invention of engines.

Fact 67 - Riders traversed vast territories

For centuries, certain peoples lived almost entirely on horseback. In the vast steppes of Eurasia, they moved across immense grasslands stretching some 8,000 kilometers, from Hungary to Manchuria. In such an open world, the ability to ride fast and for long periods provided an extraordinary advantage for traveling, hunting, patrolling, and communicating.

The Scythians are among the most famous of these horse-riding peoples. They roamed the steppes of Central Asia in tribal confederations, with herds and mobile settlements. The horse allowed them to follow the seasons, find new pastures, and traverse vast expanses. Their way of life was therefore deeply dependent on movement and endurance.

Later, the Mongols demonstrated just how far this mastery could lead. Unified in the early 13th century by Genghis Khan, they built a vast empire that eventually encompassed much of China, Russia, Central Asia, and the Middle East. Without their equestrian skills, such journeys over such long distances would have been far more difficult.

Other nomadic peoples, such as the Kazakhs, also lived across vast territories thanks to the horse. Their khanate, formed in the 15th century, stretched across the steppe east of the Caspian Sea and north of the Aral Sea. In these open regions, the horse was not merely useful; it was at the center of all daily life.

When we imagine these horsemen, we must see much more than a rider galloping across the plains. We must think of entire societies organized around the horse, capable of traversing vast expanses and staying connected across them. Their history reveals a fascinating truth: with a horse, the world suddenly seemed much larger, but also much more accessible.

Fact 68 - The first ponies helped in harsh lands

Ponies aren't just small horses. They are often very sturdy, energetic, and surprisingly resilient. This resilience made them extremely useful in regions where the climate, terrain, or soil conditions made daily life difficult. In moors, mountains, or windy islands, their modest size often proved to be a real advantage.

In these challenging environments, ponies helped carry loads, pull small carts, or navigate difficult terrain. Britannica notes that ponies have long been used to haul loads and carry packages. Their compact build, sure-footedness, and endurance made them valuable companions for humans.

Certain breeds exemplify this adaptation perfectly. The Haflinger, for example, is described by Britannica as a mountain pony—robust, hardy, and versatile—used for farm work, pulling, and carrying loads. Other ponies from northern Europe, such as the Shetland, Highland, and Fell, are also known for their resilience in demanding environments.

Their strength did not come solely from their muscles. Their calmness, intelligence, and ability to thrive in harsh conditions were just as important. In regions where large horses were sometimes less practical, ponies could move forward, carry loads, and hel s without being daunted by the terrain. Their small size thus often concealed immense courage.

When we see a pony, we sometimes think of it first as a smaller, gentler animal. Yet in many difficult regions, it has been a true hero of everyday life. Thanks to its sturdiness and incredible endurance, it has rendered great service for a very long time. Behind its small frame, therefore, lies a story of strength, adaptability, and perseverance.

Fact 69 - The horseshoe improved horses' lives

For a very long time, many horses worked on hard roads, rocky paths, and rough terrain. Under these conditions, their hooves could wear down more quickly. The horseshoe then provided invaluable help. Attached to the bottom of the hoof, it protected it from wear and allowed the horse to continue its work more comfortably.

A horse's hoof is sturdy, but it isn't indestructible. When a horse pulls a cart, plows a field, or travels long distances, its feet are put under a lot of strain. The horseshoe acts a bit like a protective sole. It limits wear on rough surfaces and helps keep the hoof in better condition over time.

The horseshoe wasn't just for protection. It could also provide better traction and stability. For a working horse, this mattered greatly. Better footing allowed the horse to pull, turn, or move forward with greater confidence. On certain roads or for certain tasks, this small metal object truly transformed the quality of daily work.

This invention is very old. Britannica notes that horseshoes likely appeared as early as Roman times, and the British Museum also houses artifacts related to this history, such as temporary hoof protectors used in the Romano-British world. This shows that humans have long sought ways to better protect horses' feet.

When we think of the great workhorses of the past, we often imagine their strength or patience. Yet part of their success lay right at the bottom, under their hooves. The horse shoe helped countless animals work on difficult terrain with greater protection. This small metal detail thus had an immense impact on their daily lives.

Fact 70 - In ancient paintings, the horse matters

Long before history books, humans left images on cave walls. Among the animals depicted, the horse appears very often. This shows that it already held an important place in their eyes and in their world. If it was painted over and over again, it was surely not by chance, but because it mattered a great deal.

In the Lascaux Cave in France, numerous prehistoric paintings depict animals, and horses feature prominently. The Encyclopædia Britannica even explains that the cave contains approximately 600 paintings and drawings of animals. This repeated presence proves that the artists of old observed horses closely and deemed them worthy of being depicted.

The Chauvet Cave, also in France, offers another impressive example. The French Ministry of Culture describes a famous "Panel of Horses" where several horse heads are drawn with great skill. These works are very ancient and already display an astonishing sense of movement, form, and observation. The horse was thus already a major subject of prehistoric art.

These paintings were likely not merely decorative. Experts believe they often held symbolic significance, important to the human groups of the time. The fact that horses appear so frequently in these images suggests they held a prominent place in the imagination, attention, or lives of prehistoric humans, even if not everything has been fully explained yet.

When we look at a horse painted thousands of years ago, we realize that this animal already fascinated humans long before the invention of writing. Its silhouette already graced the walls of caves, just as it would later grace the pages of history. These ancient images tell us something magnificent: the bond between humans and horses is so ancient that it began almost deep within the stone.

Chapter 8 : Breeds and Surprising Differences

Fact 71 - A Pony Is a Small Horse, Not a Baby

Many people believe that a pony is simply a young horse, much like a puppy is a young dog. In reality, that is not the case at all. A baby horse is called a foal. A pony, on the other hand, is an adult of a specific type, small in stature but with a fully developed, complete horse's body.

The main difference between a horse and a pony is primarily the height at the withers—that is, the height measured between the shoulders. Generally, a pony is smaller than a horse. However, height isn't the only factor to consider. A pony's body is also often more compact, with a sturdy build and strong legs.

Ponies are famous for their surprising strength. Even though they are smaller, they can be very resilient, brave, and energetic. Many live in harsh regions, with wind, rugged terrain, or cold winters. Their smaller size then becomes an advantage. It helps them conserve energy and move with agility over difficult terrain.

There are several breeds of ponies, such as the Shetland, the Connemara, and the Welsh. Each has its own appearance, temperament, and talents. Some are very lively, others calmer. Many are valued for their intelligence and sturdiness. They are therefore not unfinished horses. They are true equines, with their own qualities and their own history.

The next time you see a pony, don't mistake it for a horse that hasn't grown up yet. Instead, see it as a champion in a compact form. Behind its small size often lies great endurance, a strong personality, and plenty of ingenuity. The pony thus proves that you can be small without being a baby or lacking talent.

Fact 72 - The Arabian horse is famous for its endurance

Among the many horse breeds, the Arabian horse is one of the most famous in the world. It is admired for its elegant silhouette, its lively gaze, and above all for a very special quality: its endurance.

This means it can cover long distances while maintaining its energy for a long time. This reputation has followed it for a very long time.

The Arabian Horse Association explains that the Arabian horse is considered one of the best breeds for long distances, thanks to its endurance and stamina. This isn't just a nice way of putting it. In activities involving long journeys, this breed is often particularly valued for its ability to keep going without tiring too quickly.

This quality is particularly evident in endurance riding, an official discipline described by the International Equestrian Federation as a long-distance competition that tests the horse's speed and endurance, as well as the rider's ability to manage their effort. In this type of event, the Arabian horse often excels.

Its talent does not rest on a single trait. It often combines good pacing, great stamina, and a temperament capable of remaining steady over a long course. It is not a horse of a single burst of speed. Rather, it is a champion of endurance, capable of moving forward again and again with consistency and intelligence.

When we talk about the Arabian horse, we think of much more than just an elegant breed. We think of a true long-distance specialist, admired for its ability to keep going where others tire more quickly. Its remarkable endurance teaches us a valuable lesson about the animal world: sometimes, true prowess isn't about going the fastest, but about going far with consistency.

Fact 73 - The Friesian impresses with its long black mane

The Friesian horse often draws everyone's attention the moment it appears. Its black coat, proud bearing, and great elegance give it an almost majestic air. But what immediately stands out is its long, dark mane, often thick and wavy. It frames its neck with great panache and further reinforces the impression of calm power it exudes.

The Friesian originates from the Netherlands, more specifically from the province of Friesland, from which it takes its name. This ancient breed has been known for centuries. It has long been prized for its beauty, strength, and remarkable presence. With its solid build, powerful limbs, and expressive head, the Friesian possesses a silhouette that is highly recognizable among the world's horses.

Its mane is not its only striking feature. The Friesian also often has a long black tail and feathering—the hair that hangs down around the lower legs. The overall effect is very theatrical, almost as if it were dressed for a grand parade. Yet behind this spectacular appearance lies an energetic, spirited, and generally very attentive horse.

This breed is often admired in shows, parades, and certain equestrian disciplines because it combines beauty and presence. When the Friesian moves, its mane accompanies each step and accentuates the grace of its movement. It sometimes looks as though it is dancing with the horse. This detail makes its silhouette even more lively and contributes greatly to its unique charm.

When you see a Friesian moving forward with its long black mane flowing along its neck, you understand why it is so fascinating. It seems to come from another time, yet remains very real. Its beauty comes not only from its color, but from the harmony of its entire silhouette. In this horse, elegance and strength go hand in hand.

Fact 74 - The Shire is one of the largest horses

The Shire is a horse that immediately impresses with its size. When standing next to a human, it often seems immense, almost like a calm giant from another age. This breed is among the largest in the world. With its massive body, broad chest, and long, powerful legs, it gives off a truly spectacular impression of quiet strength.

Native to England, the Shire has long been bred as a draft horse. This means it was primarily used to pull heavy loads. Its large size was therefore not just impressive to look at; it was very useful for work. Thanks to its power, it could move carts, equipment, or other heavy loads with remarkable patience.

Despite its giant appearance, the Shire is often appreciated for its calm temperament. It moves with dignity, without needing to show off its strength at every turn. It is this contrast that makes it fascinating. At first glance, one sees a massive horse, but one often discovers an attentive, composed, and cooperative animal. Its grandeur is thus generally accompanied by a beautiful gentleness.

The Shire is also recognizable by certain elegant details. It often has feathering—those long hairs around the lower legs—which further enhance its majestic appearance. Its sturdy neck, powerful back, and steady gait complete this impressive silhouette. In this horse, everything seems designed to unite power and stability within a single, large body.

When you encounter a Shire for the first time, you quickly understand why it makes such an impression. It is not just a large horse. It is a true colossus of the equine world, built for strength yet capable of great serenity. Its presence reminds us that an animal can be gigantic without losing its nobility, calm, and beautiful elegance.

Fact 75 - The Shetland is small but incredibly sturdy

The Shetland pony is one of the smallest ponies in the world, but don't let its size fool you. Beneath its compact appearance lies a very sturdy animal, capable of withstanding harsh conditions. Its stocky build, strong legs, and boundless energy make it a true champion of resilience, far more powerful than one might imagine at first glance.

It originates from the Shetland Islands, north of Scotland, where the climate is often cold, windy, and harsh. To survive in such an environment, this pony has developed a body perfectly adapted to its surroundings. Its coat thickens in winter, its silhouette helps retain body heat, and its resilient nature allows it to endure conditions that other animals would find more challenging.

The Shetland pony is also known for its surprising strength. Although small, it can pull or carry loads that are proportionally large for its size. This is a quality that was once very useful. Its power does not come from a massive build, but from a compact, muscular body perfectly designed to conserve energy while remaining efficient.

Its temperament also plays a role in this impression of sturdiness. The Shetland pony is often lively, strong-willed, and self-assured. It is not easily daunted by challenges. This combination of small stature, great resilience, and a strong-willed nature makes it a very unique pony. It demonstrates that one can be modest in height yet immense in capability.

When you see a Shetland pony, you might think it's just an adorable little horse. Yet its history and physique tell a much bigger story. It is the perfect example that, in nature, size isn't everything. With this pony, robustness isn't measured in centimeters, but in courage, endurance, and hidden strength.

Fact 76 - The Appaloosa is often recognized by its spotted coat

Among the most easily recognizable horses, the Appaloosa holds a special place. Its appearance immediately catches the eye, as its coat often displays very distinctive spots. These patterns can resemble small dots, large light spots, or more subtle designs. Each Appaloosa seems almost to be wearing a garment painted by nature.

Not all Appaloosa coats are exactly the same. Some have their hindquarters covered in spots, others have a more extensive pattern, and a few have only a few visible markings. This variety makes each horse unique. Yet, even with these differences, the breed as a whole remains highly recognizable. You quickly notice that it doesn't quite look like other horses.

Their coat isn't their only distinctive feature, either. Many Appaloosas also have spotted skin around the muzzle or eyes, as well as hooves that are sometimes striped. The white of their eyes is often more visible than in other horses. All these details combined reinforce their unique appearance and make their silhouette even easier to identify.

The Appaloosa is also known for being an energetic, intelligent, and versatile horse. It's not just a pleasure to look at. It also possesses genuine qualities of movement and character. Its popularity therefore stems from both its spectacular appearance and its abilities. In this breed, the uniqueness of the coat is often accompanied by a very interesting temperament.

When you look at an Appaloosa, you get the impression that nature had fun creating an artistic horse. Its spots catch the eye, but they also tell a story of diversity and beauty. No two patterns are exactly alike. That's why the Appaloosa always gives the impression of being both recognizable and completely unique.

Fact 77 - The Thoroughbred was bred for speed

The Thoroughbred is one of the best-known horses when it comes to racing. This is no coincidence. This breed was developed in England specifically to run fast and well. For a long time, breeders selected the fastest and highest-performing horses for breeding. Gradually, this shaped a horse exceptionally gifted for speed.

Its physique clearly reflects this specialization. The Thoroughbred typically has a slender build, a deep chest, and legs built to produce long, efficient strides. Britannica explains that its limbs have short bones in certain areas, which promotes a long, easy stride. Its entire body seems designed to move forward quickly with power and agility.

The history of this breed is equally fascinating. Britannica notes that its origins trace back to crossbreeding in England using Eastern horses, particularly Arabians and Barb horses, followed by rigorous selection encouraged by race-loving . Three famous stallions—the Byerly Turk, the Darley Arabian, and the Godolphin Barb—rank among its most important ancestors.

The Thoroughbred is now used worldwide for racing and has also been used to improve other breeds. Its reputation is based not only on its speed, but also on its ability to sustain a sustained effort on the track. It is therefore not just a horse that is fast for a few seconds. It is a true athlete bred for performance.

When you see an English Thoroughbred racing, you are witnessing the result of a long history of selective breeding. Its speed did not appear by magic. It has been sought after, developed, and passed down through generations. This horse thus offers a striking insight into nature and human history: sometimes, speed becomes almost an art form, crafted with patience.

Fact 78 - The Camargue is born dark and turns white

The Camargue horse is famous for its very light coat, which gives it an elegant and luminous appearance. Yet it is not born that way. At birth, the Camargue foal has a dark coat, often black, dark brown, or very dark gray. This contrast is quite surprising, as the horse we admire as an adult seems almost as if it had stepped straight out of a white cloud.

As it grows, its coat gradually changes. It is not a sudden change, but a slow transformation that takes place over months, then years. The coat gradually lightens until it becomes very light gray, almost white. This phenomenon gives the impression that the horse changes color over time, as if light were gently settling upon it.

This evolution is characteristic of a gray coat. In gray horses, the number of light-colored hairs increases with age. The Camargue often follows this pattern. Even though it appears white as an adult, its skin remains dark beneath the coat. It is therefore not a white horse in the strict sense, but a gray horse that has become very light in color.

This change makes the Camargue even more fascinating. You can almost read its age in the evolution of its coat. The dark " " foal of yesterday gradually becomes the light-colored horse that many first imagine when this breed is mentioned. It is a beautiful surprise of nature, transforming its appearance without detracting from its identity.

Once you discover this secret, you see the Camargue in a different light. Its light coat doesn't just speak to its beauty; it also tells its story. It shows that a horse can change significantly as it grows while remaining the same brave and sturdy animal. In the Camargue, color becomes almost a visible adventure, written on its coat year after year.

Fact 79 - Some breeds pull, others run better

Not all horses were bred to do the same things. Over time, humans observed their qualities and favored certain characteristics depending on their needs. Thus, some breeds became very strong for pulling heavy loads, while others were chosen for their speed, lightness, and ability to run fast over long strides.

Draft horses, such as the Shire or the Percheron, have broad bodies, powerful muscles, and great strength. Their chests are broad, their legs are sturdy, and their gait exudes stability. These horses were very useful for pulling carts, working in the fields, or moving heavy objects. Their power made all the difference in difficult tasks.

Conversely, breeds like the English Thoroughbred were bred for speed. Their build is slimmer, their legs longer, and their strides very extended. Their entire body seems built for speed. They cover a lot of ground with each stride and display great energy, making them particularly impressive in races.

Between these two broad types, there are also horses capable of doing a bit of both, or of excelling in other areas such as endurance, jumping, or working on difficult terrain. Each breed thus tells a different story. Its build, temperament, and way of moving reveal what it has been specifically bred for over generations.

When comparing a large draft horse and a racehorse, it quickly becomes clear that not all horses are built for the same purpose. One resembles a quiet force capable of moving mountains, the other a living arrow ready to spring into action. This diversity makes the world of horses even more fascinating, rich, and full of surprises.

Fact 80 - Body shape varies by horse breed

When we think of horses, we often imagine a large animal with a mane, four sturdy legs, and a beautiful neck. Yet their bodies can vary greatly depending on the breed. Some are tall and massive, others slender and light. You only need to compare a few to see that nature, aided by humans, has created an astonishing variety of silhouettes.

Draft horses, for example, often have a broad body, a powerful chest, and very sturdy legs. They are built for strength and work. In contrast, racehorses generally have a slimmer silhouette, with long limbs and a more slender build. Their bodies seem designed for speed, momentum, and long, rapid strides.

The head, neck, back, and even the hindquarters also vary greatly depending on the breed. Some horses have a short, expressive head, while others have a more elongated profile. In some breeds, the neck appears very arched, whereas in others it remains straighter. All these details influence the horse's movement, balance, and sometimes even its abilities.

These differences did not arise by chance. For a very long time, humans selected horses based on what they did best. For pulling, carrying, racing, or covering long distances, the desired body types were not exactly the same. Gradually, these choices accentuated certain characteristics, eventually creating breeds that are instantly recognizable.

Observing a horse's body shape is therefore a bit like reading its history. Its silhouette tells the story of why its breed was developed and the qualities expected of it. That is why two horses may look alike from a distance, yet be very ly different up close. For them, the body becomes almost a living, fascinating identity card.

Chapter 9 : Birth and Growth

Fact 81 - A foal can stand up shortly after birth

For a horse, birth already marks the start of an incredible race against time. Barely into the world, the foal doesn't stay lying down for long. Generally, it tries very quickly to move its legs, straighten its body, and stand up. This speed may seem surprising, but it is vital for its survival.

Its first attempts are often clumsy and touching to watch. The foal stumbles, slips, wobbles, then bravely tries again. Its long legs seem almost too big for it. Yet it persists and makes rapid progress. In a short time, it often manages to stand for a few moments, then take its first steps near its attentive mother.

This speed is not merely an amusing feat. In the wild, a foal had to be able to follow its mother and the herd without waiting too long. A foal that remained motionless for too long would be more vulnerable. Being able to stand up early therefore allows it to stay close to the other horses, find better protection, and begin to discover the world.

Standing up quickly also helps the foal achieve an essential goal. It must find its mother's milk to feed and regain its strength. Once standing, it can move closer to her, find the right spot, and learn to suckle. Every minute counts, as these first moments are crucial for its energy, comfort, and a good start in life.

Watching a foal pull itself up onto its legs shortly after birth feels almost like witnessing a small miracle. Just yesterday, it didn't exist in the pasture, and now here it is, already ready to move forward. This feat shows just how remarkably prepared the horse is from its very first moments, with a truly impressive will to live.

Fact 82 - The mare quickly recognizes her foal by its scent

Within hours of giving birth, the mare quickly learns to recognize her foal. She doesn't rely solely on her sight to do this; her sense of smell plays a crucial role. By sniffing the foal carefully, she quickly memorizes its scent. This invisible cue then helps her distinguish her foal from the other horses around her.

We often see the mare bringing her muzzle close to the foal, sniffing it at length, and touching it gently. These gestures are not just meant to reassure the foal. They also allow her to gather a wealth of information. The foal's scent becomes, for her, a sort of natural signature—unique and invaluable in the early stages of their relationship.

This rapid recognition is very useful. The foal needs to stay close to its mother to feed, stay warm, and feel safe. For her part, the mare must know which foal to give her attention and care to. Thanks to scent, this bond forms quickly. It is a simple, discreet, and very effective way to create a genuine relationship.

Of course, smell complements other cues, such as voice, touch, and presence. But smell holds a special place, as it allows for very precise recognition. In a group of horses, this ability becomes even more important. Even if several foals are present, each mare can find her own thanks to this remarkable olfactory memory.

When we watch a mare gently tilt her head toward her newborn foal, we're witnessing much more than a tender moment. We see an essential bond forming almost in silence. Thanks to scent, the mother learns to recognize her foal very quickly. It's beautiful proof that, for horses, love also begins with the nose.

Fact 83 - The First Months Teach Life in the Herd

For a young horse, the first months of life are a real school. The foal doesn't just grow in size. It also learns to live with other horses. By staying close to its mother and the group, it gradually discovers the rules of the herd. These un , subtle lessons are very important for becoming a well-balanced horse.

Very early on, the foal observes how the adults move, rest, eat, and interact with one another. It learns to recognize body language, such as ear movements, posture, or the appropriate distance to maintain. Without much explanation, it gradually understands what is soothing, what is disruptive, and what is best avoided in communal life.

Play also helps enormously. By running with other young horses, approaching, moving away, and then returning, it tests boundaries and discovers how to interact. It learns to share space, to yield at times, and to insist a little at others. Each interaction becomes a small lesson in politeness, caution, and trust.

The mare's presence matters greatly during this period. The foal follows her, imitates her, and finds comfort in her presence. Thanks to his mother, he better understands the group's rhythm and the appropriate behaviors to adopt. She doesn't give him orders like a teacher, but she shows him every day how to live among the other horses.

When we watch a foal grow up in a herd, we're seeing much more than just a baby horse having fun. We see an attentive student, busy learning the rules of real social life. These first few months shape a large part of its social character. In horses, getting along well with others is learned very early on, almost from the very first steps.

Fact 84 - Mother's milk is the foal's first food

At the very beginning of its life, the foal depends almost entirely on its mother for nourishment. The mare's milk provides the energy and nutrients its body needs to get off to a good start. From the very first hours, it seeks to nurse. This first meal is very important, as it helps the foal regain its strength after birth.

The foal must learn quickly. It stands up on its long, still-wobbly legs, approaches its mother, and looks for the right spot to drink. It's not always perfectly easy on the first try , but it makes rapid progress. Once it finds the right spot, it can drink several times a day. Its body then grows thanks to this perfectly tailored food.

The mare's milk is precious because it perfectly meets the needs of a young horse. It helps the foal grow, get stronger, and maintain the energy needed to explore the world. It is a natural food designed for him, much like a starter pack provided by his mother to help him begin life on the right foot.

During this period, the mare also protects her foal while it nurses. She remains attentive, calm, and close to him. This moment is not only useful for feeding him. It also strengthens their bond. With each feeding, the foal finds not only nourishment and security but also the reassuring presence of his mother in his first days.

When we watch a foal drink its mother's milk, we are witnessing one of the most essential acts of its early life. This milk nourishes its body, supports its growth, and helps it get off to a good start. Behind this peaceful scene lies a great force of nature: the beginning of life often depends on simple, gentle, and indispensable care.

Fact 85 - Young horses discover the world through play

For young horses, play is much more than just a moment of fun. It is a very natural way of learning to live. By running, turning sharply, stopping suddenly, or chasing a companion, the foal tests its body and its environment. Every leap teaches it something useful for growing with greater confidence and precision.

When playing, the young horse first discovers how its long legs work. It learns to maintain its balance better, change direction quickly, and coordinate its movements. Its somewhat clumsy leaps at the start gradually become more precise. Play then acts as a joyful form of training, where every movement improves its strength, flexibility, and agility.

Play also helps it understand other horses. By approaching, backing away, chasing, or gently rubbing against a companion, it discovers the rules of group life. It learns when to insist, when to yield, and how to invite another foal to play. Without realizing it, it is already learning very important lessons about social life.

New objects, sounds, and places also become subjects of exploration. A moving shadow, a puddle of water, or a patch of different grass can pique its curiosity. By playing around these small novelties, it grows accustomed to the world around it. This gradual discovery helps it become more confident, more attentive, and less hesitant in the face of the unknown.

Watching a young horse play is like witnessing a real-life outdoor school. Its wild dashes, little jumps, and clumsy stops aren't just for fun. They gradually build its body, its character, and its way of living with others. For a foal, playing is already learning to become a horse.

Fact 86 - The foal learns very early on to follow its mother everywhere

From its very first days, the foal stays very close to its mother. Barely able to stand properly on its long legs, it is already trying to walk behind her or beside her. This behavior appears very early on, as it is essential for its safety. Following its mother ensures it does not end up alone and allows it to remain at the heart of the group.

At first, its steps are still hesitant. It trots, speeds up a little, then slows down so as not to lose her. Even if it seems clumsy, it makes rapid progress. By observing the mare, it learns where to go, when to stop, and how to move at the right pace. Its mother becomes a living guide for it, always moving before its eyes.

This following isn't just useful for getting around. It also helps the foal discover the world. By accompanying his mother, he gets to know the pasture, the other horses, the watering holes, and the safe spots. He also observes her reactions. If she stays calm, he understands that he can often relax. If she seems alert, he too becomes more vigilant.

Staying close to its mother also allows it to feed easily. When it is hungry, it can quickly catch up to her to drink her milk. This closeness strengthens their bond day after day. The foal therefore does not follow its mother solely out of habit. It follows her because she represents safety, food, an example, and trust all at once.

Watching a foal walk behind its mother is a very simple scene, but it already tells us a great deal. We see a young animal learning about the world by following in another's footsteps. This natural gesture shows just how much the early stages of a horse's life depend on a strong, patient, and precious bond between mother and foal.

Fact 87 - A young horse's baby teeth fall out

Just like in children, a young horse does not keep its first set of teeth for life. At first, it has baby teeth, which are smaller and suited to its early meals. Then, as it grows, these temporary teeth eventually fall out. They gradually give way to permanent teeth, which are stronger and better suited to the chewing needs of an adult horse.

This change does not happen all at once. It takes place over several years, in a fairly regular sequence. The new teeth gradually grow beneath the old ones, then take their place. This is why experts often examine a young horse's mouth to estimate its age. The teeth reveal a great deal about its transition from childhood to adulthood.

During this period, the young horse continues to chew grass, hay, and other suitable foods, while its mouth slowly transforms. It is not a dramatic upheaval at every moment, but a major change that progresses quietly. Its body is thus preparing for a life in which the teeth will have to work long hours to cut, grind, and wear down fibers every day.

The permanent teeth are larger and more durable, as the horse spends a great deal of time chewing. It therefore needs a set of teeth capable of withstanding years of work. This transition is an important sign of growth. It shows that the little foal is gradually becoming a stronger, more independent young horse, better equipped for its future life.

Looking at a young horse's teeth is a bit like reading the story of its growth hidden in its mouth. The baby teeth fall out, the new ones come in, and time leaves its mark without making a sound. This small detail reminds us of a fascinating fact: even in a large, elegant, and powerful animal, growing up involves tiny yet very important changes.

Fact 88 - The horse continues to grow for several more years

When a foal is born, it already looks tall on its long legs, but it is still far from finished growing. Its body will continue to change for several years. It will gain height, build strength, develop certain parts of its body, and improve its coordination. Becoming an adult horse therefore takes much longer than one might imagine.

Over the months, the young horse grows visibly. Its legs lengthen, its back changes shape, its neck becomes more defined, and its body gradually takes on a more balanced form. However, not everything grows at exactly the same pace. Some parts seem to develop faster than others, which sometimes gives young horses a slightly awkward appearance.

Growth isn't just about height. Bones, muscles, joints, and even the way they move continue to evolve as well. The young horse gradually becomes more stable, more powerful, and more harmonious in its movements. It learns to use its body more effectively as that body, too, slowly completes its development from the inside out.

The exact duration depends on the breed, diet, lifestyle, and each individual. Some horses appear very tall quite early on, but continue to develop in depth for quite some time. This is why a young horse should not be considered fully adult too soon. Its appearance may already be impressive, while its body is still in the process of building itself.

Watching a horse grow is witnessing a slow and fascinating transformation. The little foal becomes a slender young horse, then gradually a more solid and better-defined adult. This long growth process reminds us that nature takes its time to create a large, well-balanced animal. For a horse, becoming an adult is a patient journey, built year by year.

Fact 89 - Young horses test their balance

For young horses, running isn't just an explosion of joy. It's also a very useful way to discover what their bodies are already capable of. When they accelerate, turn sharply, or stop almost on a dime, they put their balance to the test. Each run then becomes a sort of natural exercise to help them better control their movements.

At first, their strides may seem a bit clumsy. Their legs are long, their energy is overflowing, and their whole body seems to want to go faster than their head. Yet, through repeated running, the young horse learns where to place its feet, how to hold itself better, and how to maintain stability. These repeated attempts gradually transform restlessness into coordination.

These runs also serve to build muscle and improve the coordination between the different parts of the movement. The neck aids balance, the back supports the effort, and the legs coordinate better and better. The young horse thus discovers how to slow down, change direction, and pick up speed again without losing its rhythm. It trains almost without realizing it.

When several young horses play together, this learning process becomes even richer. They chase each other, pass one another, turn at the same time, and must adjust their movements very quickly. These games teach them not only to better control their own bodies but also to react to the movements of others. Their balance is thus built through action, observation, and experience.

Watching a young horse run in a pasture is like watching a student in the midst of training. Through its joyful leaps and sudden starts, it gradually builds its agility. What looks like simple play is actually hard physical work. For a young horse, balance doesn't come from nowhere. It is discovered at full speed, stride by stride.

Fact 90 - Weaning drastically changes a foal's life

Early in life, the foal depends heavily on its mother. It drinks her milk, walks by her side, and finds comfort in her presence. Then comes an important stage called weaning. This means it gradually stops nursing. This change marks a major turning point, as it must learn to live more independently.

Weaning doesn't just change its diet. It also alters its habits, its rhythm, and its relationship with its mother. The foal begins to rely more on grass, hay, and life with other horses. It discovers that it can feed itself in other ways and spend more time exploring the world without staying glued to her.

This period requires adaptation. The foal must gain confidence, as it loses some of the comfort it has known since birth. It learns to handle more things on its own. It is also a time when the presence of other young horses or a calm environment can greatly help it navigate this change more peacefully.

Weaning plays an important role in its growth. By becoming more independent, the young horse moves toward a new stage in its life. It continues to learn the rules of the herd, develop its body, and strengthen its character. It doesn't become an adult all at once, of course, but it takes an essential step toward greater independence.

When observing a foal after weaning, one often sees a young horse beginning to find its place in the world. There is still much to learn, but it is already not quite the same. This stage shows that as it grows, the young horse gradually changes its role, with courage, flexibility, and confidence.

Chapter 10 : Records, Talents, and Curiosities

Fact 91 - Horses can sometimes sleep standing up

Seeing a horse standing still, with its eyes half-closed and its head slightly lowered, sometimes gives the impression that it is dozing without actually lying down. And this is often true. Horses can sleep standing up during part of their rest. This amazing ability allows them to relax without lying down completely, which is very practical for an animal that must remain ready to react quickly.

This secret comes from a very clever system in their legs. Thanks to a natural locking mechanism, called the supporting apparatus, certain joints can remain stable with almost no effort. The horse can then relax some of its muscles while remaining standing. We often see it rest a limb, a sign that it is quietly relaxing.

Sleeping while standing, however, does not mean that the horse spends all its nights this way. For certain deeper sleep phases, it also needs to lie down. During these times, its body relaxes further. But for short periods of light rest, staying on its feet suits it just fine. It's a smart solution that balances relaxation and alertness.

In the wild, this habit had a major advantage. A horse that is lying down takes longer to get back up than one that is already standing. By resting without lying down completely, it maintained a better chance of reacting quickly in case of danger. Even at rest, its body remained poised to protect its own safety and that of the herd.

When you see a horse standing still, almost frozen like a peaceful statue, it may not just be daydreaming. It might be taking a quick nap while standing. This amazing ability shows once again how well the horse is designed to live in a balance between calm and vigilance. Even its sleep reveals a remarkable bodily intelligence.

Fact 92 - Horses sweat to cool down

When a horse runs, trots for a long time, or works energetically, its body produces a lot of heat. Its muscles function like powerful living engines, and this activity warms the entire body. To avoid overheating, the horse uses a very effective solution: it sweats. This sweating helps lower its temperature during and after exertion.

Sweat appears on the skin, and then the air helps it evaporate. It is precisely this evaporation that carries away some of the body's heat. You could say that the horse has a sort of natural air conditioner. The more intense the exertion or the warmer the air, the more important this mechanism becomes in helping the horse maintain a comfortable temperature.

Sweat is often noticeable on the neck, shoulders, flanks, or between the legs. The coat becomes damp, sometimes even frothy in certain areas. This isn't necessarily a cause for concern. It's often a sign that the body is working to cool itself down. The horse expends energy, and its body immediately works to maintain a healthy internal balance.

But sweating doesn't just release heat. The horse also loses water and salt. That's why it needs to drink after exertion and recover calmly. Its body needs to replenish its reserves. A horse that has sweated heavily therefore requires special attention, especially when it's hot or after prolonged work.

The next time you see a horse drenched in sweat after a race or an active session, think about everything its body is doing silently. It's not just showing that it has exerted itself. It's also proving that it knows how to protect itself intelligently from the heat. Even its sweat reveals the remarkable ingenuity of its body.

Fact 93 - A horse recognizes a familiar route

A horse doesn't just walk by watching where to place its hooves. It also memorizes the paths it takes. After passing the same spot several times, it can recognize a familiar route and show that it knows where it's going. A turn, an incline, a gate, or a tree become real landmarks in the landscape for it.

This memory of the route helps it greatly to move with more confidence. On a familiar path, it often hesitates less, moves more calmly, and seems to understand more quickly what lies ahead. Its body already seems prepared. It knows where to slow down, where to turn, and sometimes even where a section requires more attention under its hooves.

The horse uses several cues to find its way along a route. It observes the contours of the terrain, notices certain objects, senses the smells of the place, and also remembers the feel of the ground. A slope, a gate, or a patch of shade can become very useful landmarks. So it's not just his sight that's at work, but his entire way of perceiving the environment.

This ability is invaluable in daily life. A horse that knows a route well may be calmer, as it has a better idea of what to expect. In a new place, it observes more closely and takes more time to understand. But once the route is memorized, it often retains it with astonishing accuracy, almost as if it were drawing a map in its head.

When you see a horse moving confidently along a path it has traveled before, you can imagine that it is gradually recalling memories of the route. It isn't just following the cues of the moment. It also recognizes landmarks it has stored in its memory. This is yet another sign that the horse is an attentive, observant animal—and far smarter than it appears.

Fact 94 - Horses can have useful whiskers

Around the muzzle and sometimes near the eyes, horses have long, slightly stiff hairs often called whiskers. Their real name is vibrissae. These hairs aren't just for decoration. They're very useful for helping the horse better sense what's right next to it, especially in areas it can't see well.

Horses have a very wide field of vision, but right in front of their noses, they have trouble distinguishing certain details. Their whiskers make up for this small shortcoming. When they brush against an object, a plant, a barrier, or the edge of a bucket, they send very precise information. The horse then better understands the shape, distance, or position of whatever is in front of it.

These sensitive hairs also help when the horse is searching for food. By bringing its muzzle close to the ground, it can better sense what it's touching even before grabbing the grass with its lips. The whiskers thus play a role in a kind of tactile exploration. They complement the work of the nose, lips, and eyes to make movements more precise.

Their usefulness becomes even clearer in dark places or when the horse needs to inspect something very closely. In these moments, the whiskers act a bit like tiny sensors. They help the horse avoid certain unwanted contact and better understand its surroundings without needing to see every detail perfectly.

The next time you look at a horse's muzzle, pay attention to those inconspicuous hairs that are sometimes barely noticeable. Yet they hide a very practical talent. Thanks to them, the horse senses the world right in front of it better. Even its whiskers show just how well-designed, precise, and full of amazing tricks its body is.

Fact 95 - Horses often sense rain or a downpour

Sometimes horses seem to sense the coming of rain even before the first drops fall. They lift their heads, become more alert, or sometimes seek a more sheltered spot. It's not magic. Their bodies and highly developed senses often allow them to notice small changes in the air long before humans do.

Horses can perceive variations that we barely notice, such as humidity, wind strength, certain odors, or changes in atmospheric pressure. These tiny clues gradually transform the atmosphere around them. Thanks to their sensitive nostrils, attentive ears, and experience, they understand that a change in the weather is brewing.

In a pasture, you sometimes see several horses reacting almost simultaneously. They move around, huddle closer together, or change their behavior before a storm or a downpour. This shows that they are highly attuned to their environment. They can't predict the weather like a forecast, of course, but they often sense that a change is coming.

This sensitivity also stems from their ancient way of life. For thousands of years, horses lived outdoors, exposed to wind, rain, cold, and heat. Quickly detecting a change in the weather could help them position themselves better, conserve energy, or stay more comfortable. Their vigilance has thus developed alongside nature.

When you see a horse suddenly become very alert even though the sky still seems calm, it may have already sensed something you haven't noticed. Its body picks up on messages invisible to most humans. This is yet another fascinating talent of the horse, that keen observer of the world capable of sensing the whims of the sky.

Fact 96 - Some horses excel at precise exercises

Not all horses excel solely through their speed or strength. Some impress most of all with their precision. This means they can perform very exact movements with great control and attention. In certain exercises, they place their feet in the right spot, turn at the right moment, and respond to very subtle cues with remarkable accuracy.

This precision requires excellent coordination. The horse must be fully aware of its body position, maintain its balance, and adjust every movement. Its back, neck, legs, and even its gaze work together. Nothing is left to chance. A slight shift in weight or a subtle change in direction can make all the difference.

We see this quality in exercises where the horse must follow a path, go around an obstacle, stop exactly at a certain spot, or perform very precise movements. To succeed, it is not en enough to be obedient. The horse must also be attentive, calm, and capable of repeating a movement consistently. It is truly a work of finesse.

All horses can learn to become more precise, but some seem particularly gifted at it. Their temperament, concentration, and way of moving help them a great deal. A horse that's too impatient risks losing its composure, while an attentive horse takes the time to position its body more effectively. Precision, therefore, comes as much from the mind as from the movement.

When you watch a horse perform a precise exercise, you discover another kind of talent. It doesn't seek to impress with speed, but with mastery. Every step seems deliberate, every movement is spot-on. This elegance of detail reveals something fascinating: in horses, power can also be expressed through calmness, finesse, and precision.

Fact 97 - Ponies carry more than you'd think given their size

When we see a pony, we often think it's too small to perform strenuous tasks. Yet its size can be deceiving. Many ponies are capable of carrying a load that's quite substantial relative to their body. They don't become giants, but their sturdiness often surprises those who judge them solely by their appearance.

This strength comes from their compact build. Ponies often have a solid body, a short back, sturdy limbs, and efficient musculature. Their build helps them withstand exertion with stability. It's not a matter of height, but of proportions. A small, well-built body can sometimes prove more powerful than one might imagine.

However, one must remain reasonable. Carrying more than one might think does not mean carrying just anything. Like all horses, ponies have limits that must be respected for their comfort and health. Their relative strength is remarkable, but it also depends on their age, physical condition, and how the load is distributed.

This quality has been of great service in many regions. Ponies have carried children, transported objects, or helped in difficult terrain where their small size became an advantage. They navigated narrow spaces, maintained good balance, and worked with courage. Their modest appearance thus often concealed a true capacity for effort.

The pony reminds us of a very simple and very true lesson. You cannot measure an animal's strength with a measuring stick alone. A small frame can conceal great endurance, balance, and power. In the pony's case, its small size does not detract from its effectiveness. On the contrary, it is sometimes part of the secret of its strength.

Fact 98 - Horses use their lips like little fingers

A horse's lips are far more dexterous than one might imagine. They are not used solely for eating. They also help the horse grasp, sort, and explore what lies before it. Thanks to them, a horse can pluck a specific blade of grass, touch an object, or examine something with great delicacy, almost as if it had little fingers at the tip of its nose.

When grazing, the horse uses its lips to select the grass before cutting it with its front teeth. They are flexible, mobile, and very sensitive. This allows it to choose exactly what it wants to eat. It doesn't just take anything at random. Its lips work like tiny tools capable of feeling, pushing, pulling, and guiding.

This dexterity also serves it well outside of mealtimes. A horse can use its lips to gently rummage through hay, grab a light object, or explore a clasp, a rope, or the rim of a bucket. Often, it starts by touching with its lips before deciding what to do. It's a discreet but very effective way to discover the world around it.

Their high sensitivity makes them particularly useful for delicate tasks. Since a horse's vision is less clear right in front of its nose, its lips help it better understand what it's touching. They thus complement the work of its whiskers, sense of smell, and memory. Its muzzle then becomes a true zone of exploration, always in motion and full of precision.

The next time you see a horse delicately picking something up, take a close look at its lips. You'll realize they're almost as useful to it as hands. Beneath their simple appearance lies an astonishing dexterity. In horses, even the most ordinary movements reveal unexpected finesse and a very intelligent way of using their bodies.

Fact 99 - Horses sometimes roll around for their own good

When a horse lies down and then rolls on the ground, you might think it's just having fun. In reality, this action often serves a real purpose. By rubbing its body against the earth, sand, or dry grass, it helps keep its skin and coat comfortable. This behavior is therefore part of its natural grooming routine.

Rolling around primarily helps relieve minor discomforts. After sweating, after a rain shower, or during times when insects are abundant, the horse often enjoys this thorough rubbing of its entire body. It can help the horse dry off a bit, remove dirt, or soothe certain unpleasant sensations on the skin. It's a true moment of comfort.

The ground acts somewhat like a large natural brush. By rolling from one side to the other, the horse rubs its neck, back, flanks, and sometimes even its hindquarters. This movement can also help restore the coat's natural order after exertion. Despite its amusing appearance, this rolling serves a very practical purpose.

This behavior also contributes to the horse's overall well-being. A relaxed horse often chooses a spot where it feels safe before lying down to roll. Since it puts itself in a more vulnerable position, it prefers a quiet, familiar place. This shows that, in addition to caring for its skin, it is also seeking a true moment of relaxation.

The next time you see a horse rolling energetically, look at the scene differently. It's not just a funny somersault in the dust. It's also a smart way to take care of its body. Even in this big, joyful, and somewhat theatrical movement, the horse shows once again how well it knows how to use nature to its advantage.

Fact 100 - Every horse has a unique personality

When observing several horses, you quickly notice that they don't all react the same way. One approaches right away, while another stays a little at a distance. One likes to explore, while another prefers to watch for a long time first. Just like humans, every horse has its own way of being, with its own habits, preferences, and unique reactions.

Some horses are very curious. They stick their noses out, want to sniff new objects, and always seem ready to discover something. Others are more cautious and take the time to observe before acting. There are also calm, playful, sensitive, energetic, or very set-in-their-ways horses. No two are exactly alike.

This personality depends on several factors. Part of it undoubtedly comes from their innate nature, but experience also plays a major role. A horse that grew up in a calm environment or frequently experiences reassuring situations may become more confident. Another, more often startled or anxious, may remain more reserved. Their personal history thus leaves its mark on their behavior.

In a herd, these differences are very evident. Some horses readily take the lead, while others follow more discreetly. A few calm the group with their composure, while others sound the alarm more quickly. This mix of personalities enriches life in the herd and shows that each horse brings something unique to those around them.

When you get to know a horse, you discover much more than a breed, a size, or a color. You encounter a true personality. This unique character makes every relationship different and every horse memorable. That is why enthusiasts often speak of them as individuals in their own right. Beneath the same elegant silhouette, there are a hundred ways to be a horse, and no two are quite alike.

Conclusion

You've just completed an amazing journey into the heart of the horse world. By discovering their mobile ears, ingenious hooves, gaits, memory, and life in herds, you've seen that a horse is much more than a fast and elegant animal. It is a sensitive, clever, attentive being, wonderfully adapted to its natural environment.

Each fact has shown you a detail that sometimes seemed very small, but which tells a great story. A whisker, a posture, a tooth, a stride, or a simple whinny can reveal treasures of science, history, and intelligence. With horses, even what seems unremarkable can become a fascinating discovery when you take the time to observe.

You now know that there are very different kinds of horses: sturdy ponies, brave foals, and breeds with astonishing talents. You've also discovered that their bodies, their temperaments, and their way of life tell an ancient story, connected to both nature and humans. This makes every horse unique, almost like a one-of-a-kind encounter.

Close this book with a simple yet precious insight: the more closely you observe a horse, the more wonders you'll discover. Perhaps one day you'll come across a horse in a meadow, a pony on a path, or a foal near its mother. At that moment, you'll see more than just a beautiful animal. You'll recognize a champion of surprises.

Marc Dresqui

Quiz

1) What can a horse's teeth help estimate?
a)   The horse's top speed
b)   The horse's age
c)   The horse's favorite color
d)   The exact length of its tail

2) What feature of a horse helps make its movements more fluid?
a)   It has two tails
b)   It doesn't have a collarbone like humans
c)   It has metal hooves
d)   It has six legs

3) Why can a horse neigh?
a)   Only to ask for food
b)   Only to scare other animals
c)   To call out, show emotion, or react to a situation
d)   To fall asleep faster

4) How can a horse warn others of danger without making a sound?
a)   By raising its head, pricking up its ears, and changing its posture
b)   By tapping its hooves to make music
c)   By closing its eyes very tightly
d)   By lying down immediately on the ground

5) Why do horses like to live with other horses?
a)   Because they want to learn how to climb trees
b)   Because living in a group helps them feel safer and more at ease
c)   Because they don't know how to walk alone
d)   Because they always prefer to sleep standing up together

6) How do you gain a horse's trust?
a)   By shouting very loudly to make it obey
b)   By moving forward with patience, gentleness, and consistency
c)   By changing your approach every day
d)   By surprising it often to get it used to it

7) What allows a horse to turn very quickly without falling?
   a)   Thanks to its balance and the coordination of its entire body
   b)   Thanks to its hidden wings
   c)   Thanks to its tail pushing against the ground
   d)   Thanks to its closed eyes

8) What does a horse do when the ground gets slippery?
   a)   It jumps higher to avoid the ground
   b)   It shortens its strides and moves more carefully
   c)   It closes its eyes to concentrate
   d)   It runs faster to get across more quickly

9) Why do a horse's teeth wear down naturally?
   a)   Because it bites on stones every day
   b)   Because it chews on fiber-rich grass and hay for a long time
   c)   Because it never drinks water
   d)   Because its teeth fall out every week

10) Why does a horse graze slowly for hours on end?
   a)   Because it always forgets to finish its meal
   b)   Because its body is designed to eat little by little and almost
        continuously
   c)   Because it prefers to sleep while eating
   d)   Because it never likes fresh grass

11) What helps some horses tolerate the cold well?
   a)   A thick winter coat that keeps heat close to the body
   b)   Fins hidden under their skin
   c)   Running all night without stopping
   d)   A coat that's always wet from the rain

12) How does a horse often find the best path on difficult terrain?
   a)   By closing its eyes to concentrate better
   b)   By observing the ground and choosing the most passable
        spot
   c)   By jumping randomly in all directions
   d)   By always following the birds in the sky

13) Why did some civilizations breed horses specifically for war?
   a)   So they could learn to swim while wearing armor
   b)   To have brave, fast mounts suited for combat

c)   So they would pull only festive carts
d)   So they would become smaller than ponies

14) What does the frequent presence of horses in prehistoric cave paintings indicate?
a)   That prehistoric humans considered the horse important
b)   That horses could paint on their own
c)   That caves served as giant stables
d)   That horses lived exclusively underground

15) Why is the Shetland pony considered very sturdy?
a)   Because it is very large and very heavy
b)   Because it has a compact, sturdy body well-suited to harsh conditions
c)   Because it lives only in heated stables
d)   Because it runs faster than any other horse in the world

16) Why does the body shape of horses vary by breed?
a)   Because all horses grow randomly
b)   Because over time, humans have selected horses suited to different roles
c)   Because horses change breeds every winter
d)   Because their silhouette depends only on the color of their coat

17) What is the main purpose of play for young horses?
a)   To learn how to grow, move better, and understand other horses
b)   To fall asleep faster in the pasture
c)   To change the color of their coat
d)   To avoid eating grass

18) What does weaning mean for a foal?
a)   That it gradually learns to stop suckling and become more independent
b)   That it starts flying with its mother
c)   That its coat color changes immediately
d)   That it sleeps all day without moving

19) How can a horse sense that a change in the weather is approaching?
a)   Thanks to its senses, which detect humidity, wind, smells, and air pressure

b) Thanks to a weather map hidden in the pasture
c) Thanks to its hooves that glow in the dark
d) Thanks to a secret song it hears in the clouds

20) Why can we say that every horse has a unique personality?
a) Because they all react exactly the same way
b) Because every horse has its own habits, preferences, and ways of reacting
c) Because only black horses have a personality
d) Because a horse changes its personality every hour

Answers

1) What can a horse's teeth help determine?
Correct answer: b) The horse's age

2) What unique feature of a horse helps make its movements more fluid?
Correct answer: b) It does not have a collarbone like humans

3) Why might a horse neigh?
Correct answer: c) To call out, show emotion, or react to a situation

4) How can a horse warn others of danger without making a sound?
Correct answer: a) By raising its head, pricking up its ears, and changing its posture

5) Why do horses like to live with other horses?
Correct answer: b) Because living in a group helps them feel safer and more at ease

6) How do you gain a horse's trust?
Correct answer: b) By moving forward patiently, gently, and steadily

7) What allows a horse to turn very quickly without falling?
Correct answer: a) Thanks to its balance and the coordination of its entire body

8) What does a horse do when the ground becomes slippery?
Correct answer: b) It shortens its strides and moves more carefully

9) Why do a horse's teeth wear down naturally?
Correct answer: b) Because it chews fiber-rich grass and hay for long periods of time

10) Why does a horse graze slowly for long hours?
Correct answer: b) Because its body is designed to eat little by little and almost continuously

11) What helps some horses tolerate the cold well?

Correct answer: a) A thick winter coat that keeps heat close to the body

12) How does a horse often find the best path on difficult terrain?

Correct answer: b) By observing the ground and choosing the most passable spot

13) Why did some civilizations breed horses specifically for war?

Correct answer: b) To have brave, fast mounts suited for combat

14) What does the frequent appearance of horses in prehistoric cave paintings indicate?

Correct answer: a) That prehistoric humans considered the horse important

15) Why is the Shetland pony considered very hardy?

Correct answer: b) Because it has a compact, sturdy body well-suited to harsh conditions

16) Why does the body shape of horses vary by breed?

Correct answer: b) Because over time, humans have selected horses suited to different roles

17) What is the main purpose of play for young horses?

Correct answer: a) To learn how to grow, move more effectively, and understand other horses

18) What does weaning mean for a foal?

Correct answer: a) That it gradually learns to stop suckling and become more independent

19) How can a horse sense that a change in weather is approaching?

Correct answer: a) Through its senses, which detect humidity, wind, smells, and air pressure

20) Why can we say that every horse has a unique personality?

Correct answer: b) Because every horse has its own habits, preferences, and ways of reacting